NAPOLEON III
AND THE RHINE

NAPOLEON III AND THE RHINE

THE ORIGIN OF THE WAR OF 1870-1871

BY

HERMANN ONCKEN

WITH AN INTRODUCTION BY
FERDINAND SCHEVILL

TRANSLATED BY EDWIN H. ZEYDEL

NEW YORK / RUSSELL & RUSSELL

REISSUED, 1967, BY RUSSELL & RUSSELL
A DIVISION OF ATHENEUM HOUSE, INC.
BY ARRANGEMENT WITH ALFRED A. KNOPF, INC.
L. C. CATALOG CARD NO.: 66-24743

PRINTED IN THE UNITED STATES OF AMERICA

TRANSLATOR'S NOTE

The material herewith published is a translation of volume I, pages 1–120, of the three-volume work "Die Rheinpolitik Kaiser Napoleons III. von 1863 bis 1870 und der Ursprung des Krieges von 1870–71" (Stuttgart, Berlin, and Leipzig, 1926) by Hermann Oncken, professor of history in the University of Berlin. This material serves in the original as the author's commentary upon the official documents which comprise the rest of the three volumes. The originals of these heretofore unpublished documents, which have here been interpreted in a masterly fashion by Professor Oncken, were discovered by him in the following places: Haus-, Hof- und Staatsarchiv, Vienna; Kriegsarchiv, Vienna; Auswärtiges Amt, Berlin; Geheimes Staatsarchiv, Munich; Staatsarchiv, Stuttgart; General-Landesarchiv, Karlsruhe; and in the unpublished memoirs of Count Vitzthum. There can be no doubt that Professor Oncken's scholarly work throws more light upon the policies of Napoleon III in their relation to the genesis of the War of 1870–1871 than all hitherto published sources and discussions combined.

E. H. Z.

FOREWORD

THE DISARMAMENT to which all the powers of Europe are committed by the Treaty of Versailles, and which has been repeatedly recognized by the League of Nations as one of its leading purposes, has thus far made no headway. The reason is that the victorious powers in the World War, and none more persistently than France, have raised a prior issue: they have declared that before they will consent to disarmament they must have security. Security is a fair word and connotes to the innocent mind something to which every nation on earth, whether large or small, has a right to aspire. The question arises, however, whether diplomats and politicians are in the habit of using words innocently and according to their common meaning. We have it on the authority of Talleyrand, certainly a famous diplomat and a Frenchman and wit besides, that the only confirmed use they have for words is to conceal their thoughts; hence we are justified in suspecting that when a word is given a too insistent display by a gentleman of Talleyrand's profession, it conceals a thought of an entirely different order. Let us look at France in the light of this shibboleth of security.

As a result of the Treaty of Versailles France has become the dominating military power of Europe; her continental rival, Germany, has been disarmed so effectively that she is at the mercy not only of France but of any one of even her smaller neighbors, such as Czecho-Slovakia or Poland; with these two countries, as well as with Belgium, Jugo-Slavia, and Rumania, France has close military alliances which draw a complete ring of iron around the German Reich; the whole left bank of the Rhine, together with a 50-kilometer zone along the right bank, has been demilitarized and is thereby subject to immediate seizure by France as the opening act of war; and for the present, at least, France is in military occupation of the Rhineland and for all practical purposes has the German capital, Berlin, under its guns. Nor is this all. More important, perhaps, than all of these advantages, since 1925 France has enjoyed the benefit of the Locarno treaties, which not only pledge Germany to eschew all aggression, but also assure the French Republic of active support on the part of Great Britain in case of a German breach of the peace. If the sum of these conditions does not spell security, this desirable article must be declared to be simply unobtainable on earth. This much, however, may be boldly asserted: if any other European state were given a similar array of advantages over its most dangerous neighbor and rival, it would certainly be moved to offer thanks to its Maker every hour of the day. It is reasonably clear, therefore, that France in talking about security means something that cannot be said to be covered by that word under any acceptable definition.

What France conceals behind the word security can be discovered infallibly in only one way—by appealing to history to the end of ascertaining the course of French policy toward Germany, not since 1919 or any near date, but over a span of centuries. Such an investigation will show that ever since the time of Richelieu, that is, for a period of three hundred years, France has in respect to Germany consistently held two purposes, which are the halves of but a single purpose: (1) to conquer or control all the German territory up to the left bank of the Rhine, and (2) to keep the German states disunited and thereby subject to French control. In the eyes of the French it was not permissible for their German neighbors to follow the French lead and become a nation, and they were resolved to hinder this consummation at every cost. Nevertheless in the nineteenth century the Germans, themselves a somewhat headstrong people, took up the policy of unification and made slow but consistent progress toward the goal. Rather than let them actually reach it, the French unleashed a war—the War of 1870—and lost. Victorious Germany became united, and before the passing of many years had outstripped France in population, wealth, and military power. Then came the War of 1914, and when, in 1919, defeated Germany was at the mercy of the victors, the French representatives made their appearance at the council table with nothing more or less than the old, double-barreled demand of Richelieu: the Rhineland owned or, as a second choice, controlled by France, and a Germany redissolved into a congeries of small states after the manner of the Treaty of Westphalia. So fused with the deep-down national instincts of the French people was this policy that it could go underground for a whole generation and on reappearance show an absolutely unchanged physiognomy!

Only because the United States and Great Britain refused to concur was France obliged to modify her demands and to be content with the, after all, enormous advantages secured by the Treaty of Versailles. However, to the clamorous disappointment of the French patriots, German unity remained intact and, though France acquired a vigorous military grip upon the Rhineland, she did not obtain legal title. Her chagrin has ever since been voiced in frank and unmeasured terms wherever nationalist Frenchmen are alone among themselves; but when they wish to influence the public opinion of the world they swallow their feelings and play variations on the dulcet theme, security. That security does not mean what it says is a certainty in view of the unparalleled security obtained at Versailles, the elements of which have already been enumerated. It means just one thing, clearly legible in the light of the three-hundred-year-old policy of the country: the Rhine boundary and a disunited Germany. Plainly, security in this selfish sense cannot be talked about at general diplomatic conferences; and, more plainly still, a security of this kind, which one nation gains by imposing insecurity and total dependence on another nation, is abhorrent to the current moral opinion of the world.

While the United States and Great Britain, represented at Paris in 1919 by President Wilson and Premier Lloyd George, refused to meet the French wishes in regard to Germany, they were nevertheless desirous of giving to France a very liberal measure of real advantages over her neighbor, as the Treaty of Versailles amply testifies. They were thus favorably disposed to France because they had just fought at her side a long-drawn-out, terrific war, in which France, as battle-ground, had suffered unspeakable devastation. Besides, convulsed by the same war passions, they had developed a common mind with France and created a mythology in regard to their enemy, Germany, admirably calculated to keep the fighting spirit alive and glowing among their peoples, and to discredit Germany before the world by making her appear as the enemy of all mankind. Among the commonest accusations voiced by the very effective allied propaganda was that France, an innocent victim, had within the last one hundred years been four times wantonly invaded by the ruffian, Germany—in 1814, in 1815, in 1870, and in 1914. As a commonplace of allied argument this charge was constantly voiced by all the allied delegations at Paris. Mr. Lloyd George in particular rode on it to many an oratorical climax. He and his sympathizers in every camp made it their key position in conceding to France the right to special advantages against her traditional foe.

Since nobody shifts his ground and changes his tune more frequently than the volatile Mr. Lloyd George, we are permitted to wonder where he stands at present on the issue of the "four German invasions of France in the last century." We even wonder, assuming that he may be, after all, not just a politician, whether he is not a wee bit ashamed. For the first two invasions, those of 1814 and 1815, as he knew perfectly well and could deny only because he was addressing a public which the frenzy of war had made absolutely blind to the truth, were not really invasions at all, since they were the wholly legitimate counter-moves by which the other countries of Europe at last put an end to a twenty-year aggression against them on the part of revolutionary France. The leader in this struggle against French expansion was so manifestly Great Britain that if the invasions are to be attributed to any one of the European powers, it would have to be to the island-kingdom, and the blushing Lloyd George would have to acknowledge his error and celebrate the campaigns of 1814 and 1815 as British invasions. If, in addition, we reflect that at that time there was as yet no Germany in existence, certainly not in any political sense, one-half of the famous allied formula has clean evaporated.

We come now to the third invasion, that of 1870. Let us agree at once that this was certainly a national German affair, for, although when the war with France started it was engaged in only by the northern group of German states under the leadership of Prussia, the southern states joined their northern brothers and actually consummated their long-expected political union on the battlefields of France. Every historian with a wide vision, no matter what his nationality, can interpret this war only as a last desperate attempt on the part of France to interrupt the unification process going on in Germany. The war was, naturally enough, treated apologetically by France after her defeat—the legendary explanation being put forth that it was due to nothing done or willed by the French government, but had come about solely through a base trick played by Bismarck. Here the legend fastened attention on what was called the "falsification" of the Ems dispatch as the single and exclusive reason why two great nations came to blows. In pro-French circles throughout Europe this version in the period after 1870 gained a qualified admission, until the reserve with which it was at first regarded broke down completely before the flood of anti-German sentiment which poured over the world in 1914. From 1914 on no allied politician or publicist entertained any further doubt. The guilt of Bismarck and therewith of Prussia in forcing a war on helpless France had become an axiom! Frankly dishonest about the first two invasions, Lloyd George may be conceived to have really persuaded himself of Bismarck's sole guilt in provoking the third, since it is always pleasant for a politician who has an enemy to denounce that enemy as so devilish that in the remote as well as in the immediate past his game has been to plot wars against his unsuspecting neighbors in order to spring them at last, when fully prepared, by a sudden dastardly trick. This simplification of complex historical processes, which is agreeable and perhaps even necessary to the vast majority of us blundering, unreflecting mortals, had scored an immense success in 1914, largely under Lloyd George's inspired auspices, in fixing the onus for the world cataclysm on that manifest limb of Satan, the Kaiser. Since nobody doubted the Kaiser's guilt in the latest instance, it seemed invidious not to trace William II's diabolism back to the far greater founder of the German Empire. So the allied propaganda would not have it otherwise than that Bismarck was the evil genius of Germany and Europe and had fallen in 1870 like a wolf upon France, the slumbering lamb.

And here, in once more calling the world's attention to the true circumstances attending the outbreak of the War of 1870, lies the significance of the present book. It was written by Professor Hermann Oncken of the University of Berlin, not as a self-sufficient study, but as an introduction to three weighty volumes of documents gleaned by him from the archives of Austria and Prussia, as well as from those of Bavaria and a number of other minor German states, all to the end of illustrating the German policy of Emperor Napoleon III in the period from 1863 to 1870 and of throwing light upon the diplomatic break which precipitated the war.[1] Because of its undoubted importance it has been considered desirable to publish this English version of Professor Oncken's introduction to the collection of documents, although without the documents the introduction runs some risk of being misunderstood. For while the original (called *Darstellung* by Professor Oncken) presents a summary sketch of Napoleon's tortuous policy toward the problem of German unification during the critical and culminating period 1863–1870 and refuses to blur its outlines by abundant quotation from and reference to documents, it is safe from critical attack because the evidence follows in such a flood in over 1300 close-printed pages of original diplomatic reports as to be overwhelming. The *Darstellung*, in other words, grew immediately out of the documents and is presented as their extract or elixir. This the reader of the translation should keep constantly in mind;

* The title of the German work is as follows: Die Rheinpolitik Kaiser Napoleons III von 1863 bis 1870 und der Ursprung des Krieges von 1870–71. Nach den Staatsakten von Oesterreich, Preussen und den süddeutschen Mittelstaaten. Von Hermann Oncken. Drei Bände. Deutsche Verlagsanstalt, Stuttgart, Berlin und Leipzig, 1926.

and if he is a scholar who demands the proof of every statement made or even if he is only a cultured reader moved by ordinary curiosity, he should not hesitate to resort to the documents which are written in either French or German and offer a direct view of a plot more palpitatingly exciting in some of its numerous twists and turns than a mere summary, however alive, can possibly be.

Even if this first difficulty is overcome—and it can be with a little good-will—the book will run the further risk of facing charges of partisanship because it emanates from a German. Well, let us agree that Professor Oncken *is* a partisan. No living German or Frenchman writing on an issue so passionately alive as are Franco-German relations is going to view the problem otherwise than from his national angle. Even outsiders, who have written in this field, are often so inflamed for either the French or the German side that their presentation of the crisis of 1870 and of every subsequent conflict between the two irreconcilable neighbors shows a decided leaning in one or the other direction. Is it not possible that we make entirely too much of non-partisanship and objectivity as the great desiderata for the writer of history? To be completely objective is to be as dry and colorless as an adding-machine, and that surely is a literary ideal which the historian should and the reader will resist as inhuman. What we have a right to demand of a historian is that he be honest, capable of subjecting his feelings to his understanding, trained to read documents critically, and ready to grub patiently for the facts and to form his judgment under their direction. Since Professor Oncken will be found to satisfy these requirements in their most severe formulation, he has a claim on our regard even though he does not indulge in the hypocritical pretension of rising above his nationality.

But while Professor Oncken's candid personality and high standards of scholarship merit the confidence of his readers, the reason for publishing his book in an English dress lies elsewhere. It lies in the circumstance that by tapping abundant undisclosed sources in the archives, the author was enabled to add numerous invaluable particulars to the story of Napoleon III's attitude toward the problem of German unification. Not that the earlier investigators of this diplomatic field had not made important discoveries of their own touching the way Napoleon schemed and plotted to squeeze something for himself out of the troubled German situation; but in Professor Oncken's book a curtain is for the first time pushed aside enabling us to have, as it were, a direct look into Napoleon's mind and to follow during a period of seven years (1863–1870) the crazy succession of his plans, hopes, and despairs anent the unification movement going on across the Rhine. We owe this intimate revelation of a very subtle schemer's mentality to the fact that the Austrian ambassador at Napoleon's court during the whole of this period was Prince Metternich, son of the famous chancellor, and that Metternich lived in the most intimate relationship with Napoleon and his wife, the Empress Eugenie. It may be admitted that Metternich owed this position in part to his social skill coupled with the very remarkable graces of his wife. Nevertheless, it must be insisted that he was primarily in the close confidence of the Emperor because from 1863 on Napoleon, abandoning his earlier course, tried to achieve good relations and ultimately an alliance with Austria. His object herein was to rearrange the map of Europe in such a way that when the easily foreseen clash came between Austria and Prussia for leadership in Germany, he would be able not only to shape the German issue in accordance with the French interest, but at the same time to possess himself of some convenient slice of German territory. To these suggestions Metternich, who desired passionately to get support for his own country against Prussia, lent a willing ear; and it is this gravitation of the two men toward a common purpose which, far more than personal sympathy, accounts for the close relationship between them.

However, Metternich was only an agent. He could report and recommend, but in the end he was obliged to carry out his instructions. From the published correspondence it clearly appears that Vienna treated all the proposals issuing from Napoleon dilatorily and suspiciously, refusing to forget the War of '59, or the emperor's revolutionary origin, or his devotion to the principle of nationality, necessarily disruptive of the polyglot Austrian state. In consequence Metternich was usually constrained to let Napoleon's proposals fall gently to the ground, only however, as soon as a new turn of the wheel of fortune seemed to alter the European outlook, to be invited by the undiscouraged Frenchman to pass on to Vienna a fresh proffer of his undying devotion. Every reader with a passion for detective stories or mystery plays will follow with breathless attention the vicissitudes of these Franco-Austrian alliance negotiations. Again and again they seem to be on the point of reaching a happy culmination when a renewed hesitation at Vienna dashes the cup from Napoleon's hand.

The repeated rejections of his hot suit by Vienna moved Napoleon to evolve a hardly less fascinating sub-plot. Firmly resolved to have a finger in the German pie, he was in the first instance minded, as we have seen, to work with Austria. But since Austria persistently eluded him, he turned to Prussia, and his efforts to get an alliance, coupled with a reasonable *pourboire* out of Prussia, were for a time as persistent as was his wooing of Austria. As a matter of lover's technique let us observe that he never pushed his suit with the two German maidens at the same time, but in a kind of tick-tock alternation. However, when Prussia defeated Austria in 1866 and began the reorganization of Germany without conceding the tiniest strip of German territory to France by way of "compensation," the French policy gradually stiffened; and after failing in 1867, through Prussian opposition, to get the Duchy of Luxemburg, Napoleon ceased to expect anything further from Prussia, unless it might be war. From this year onward the Emperor faced consistently toward Vienna; and the negotiations now spun with the Hapsburg monarchy, into which Italy was gradually drawn as a third partner, are sketched by Professor Oncken with the aid of innumerable hitherto unknown details and mark the climax of his book.

With the triple alliance of France, Austria, and Italy perfected, Napoleon planned to go to war and dictate peace in Berlin, certainly not to the advantage of the German nation. But before the treaty could be formally concluded, Bismarck took a hand in the hazardous game. There followed the Spanish incident, which, as the reports of Metternich make perfectly clear, Napoleon, Eugenie, and even more unflinchingly their foreign minister, the Duke of Grammont, treated from the first moment in just one way, that is, as an opportunity for putting before Prussia the simple alternative of public humiliation or war. In this inflammatory situation the significance of the Ems dispatch, which is an abbreviated, accurate account of the meeting between King William and the French ambassador, Benedetti, without a single falsifying feature, lies in the fact that Bismarck accepted the French challenge. Within the responsibility created and defined by his counterblast, Bismarck was a factor in precipitating the war.

We might ask in conclusion: does such a book as this make the much-discussed reconciliation between the French and German peoples appear less a fond hope than a delusion? Most decidedly it must remain a delusion if these peoples and their governments are going to continue to deal with each other, as they have in the past, in hypnotized surrender to the idea that one can prosper only if the other is repressed and miserable. Both have yielded too much and too consistently to a brutal predatory instinct, Germany more particularly in her period of triumph after 1870, and France in the period before 1870 and since 1919. If they can learn that the happiest relation possible among nations as well as individuals is that existing among equals who respect each others' rights and see eye to eye, in this case and in this case only may we look forward to an improvement which the whole world would welcome as a release from one of its most oppressive nightmares. Should they, however, be unable to divorce themselves from an evil tradition and stubbornly adhere to a policy, by virtue of which each couples with its own triumph the subjection of the other, we may be sure that all the elated talk about reconciliation and peace is but empty prattle and self-delusion.

FERDINAND SCHEVILL

University of Chicago
January 1, 1928

NAPOLEON III
AND THE RHINE

NAPOLEON III AND THE RHINE

Between the Germans and the French there have been sharp lines of demarcation with respect to settlement, language and customs—unmistakable and unchangeable lines surviving all transformations wrought by the eventful course of history and dating back a full millennium to the time when, after emerging from the universal empire of Charlemagne, the two nations became conscious of their political and spiritual individuality. The will to exist, displayed by each of the two peoples in contact with the other, could not be shaken. Although the basic facts of history are quite unequivocal, no such persistent encroachment of one national will upon the domain of another as that practised by the French upon the territory and people of Germany ever since the time of Richelieu and Louis XIV can be observed elsewhere in Europe. To appreciate this, we must think not only of land and people immediately affected by these inroads. The very fact that the menaced territory comprised the oldest German *Kulturland*, was bound to aggravate the problem and make it almost intolerable from the German point of view. Moreover, the strategic importance of the Rhine frontier weighed so heavily in the balance that whenever the Rhine was held by the French, the effect was felt by the whole of Germany east of the Rhine.

And so it was inevitable that the conflict caused by this antagonism should lead repeatedly to serious political and military embroilments on the part of the two nations, impelled by the irresistible force of tradition, which originating in the past experiences of great nations imperceptibly dominates even future generations. But worse than that, these conflicts between Germans and French were destined to disturb the peaceful intercourse of all the other European nations as well, so that this single frontier, which nature had not drawn deeply enough, furnished the ever-present cause for a struggle of all against all. And what had generally been regarded for several decades as belonging to the past, has now, since the outcome of the World War, been stirred up anew, so that it seems irrevocably and ominously bound up with the future of the European continent.

It is consequently a matter of general European concern, a matter of the highest historical and political importance, to subject these historical circumstances to a careful examination based upon the sources, and to investigate the reasons why the Franco-German hostility, having its roots in the Rhineland policy of the French, has broken out again in recent times, setting in motion a veritable avalanche of tragic consequences which nearly all of mankind has been called upon to bear.

I

Even the Rhineland policy of the French in the seventeenth and eighteenth centuries, which in every sense forms the basis for the political tradition now revived, is not a matter of German and French history alone. It concerns European history as a whole. For when the French, who had early achieved political unity and were blessed by nature with rich resources and favorable living conditions, set out to advance their political power toward the Rhine, they were quite conscious of the fact that they were aiming not merely at the acquisition of territory, which in itself would hardly have satisfied the nation's vital impulse, but rather at the attainment of nothing less than a position of preponderance upon the continent. Their own greatness seemed to demand their hegemony along the Rhine, in a territory which for a thousand years had been German soil. But since this position could be maintained only if the German state, weakened by internal dissolution, lacked the strength to ward off such an incursion, another unescapable consequence followed. To use an expression of Thiers it became "the great idea" of their policy consciously to bring about such a condition of impotence on the part of the German state by the shrewd device of *divide et impera*, or, where opportunity offered, to favor it by all possible means. Shortly before the outbreak of the World War a French publicist did homage to this "eternal" thought. With that naïveté which is characteristic of every virile national egoism, the French were convinced that the fate of the German neighbor state had been predestined by God and history, by nature or even by reason, to take such a turn as the purposes of the French nation required. Side by side and hand in hand the two peoples had once developed from the empire of Charles the Great into independent national units. But in the sequel the prosperity and power of the one—so at least it seemed to the French—had as their natural complement the disunity and servility of the other. And the same political thinkers who, in the political theory of France since the sixteenth century, developed the idea of a sovereign and centralized government, advocated with equal fervor the theory that the German neighbor was destined to the greatest possible decentralization. Thus the *liberté* of the German estates became a French slogan. Precisely because the hegemony of France seemed assured only by the sacrifice of the political unity and order of the neighboring state, as well as by the acquisition of the "keys to the Rhine," both were immediately claimed as an imperative necessity. That is the classical Rhineland policy of the French, which as early as the age of Louis XIV merged into one single idea three political aims, namely, a victorious advance to the Rhine, a system of intervention in the domestic affairs of Germany, and an assertion of leadership on the continent. This idea not only gratified all the desires of the national logic; it also inspired the national will with a new and hopeful promise.

In the course of time, to be sure, the official Rhineland policy passed through divers stages of development. But in reality it was only the external form of assertion, only the mode of public justification which were adapted to the varying exigencies of different ages and hence underwent certain changes. Here, too, the French proved skilful, according to Albert Sorel's striking phrase, "in enlisting an uncritical science in the service of an unscrupulous policy." While under Louis XIV historical legends and judicial fictions were set in motion to provide the king's long series of legal infractions with the semblance of justice, the great revolution, breaking with all history and all feudal rights, sought for new arguments of its own making. The theory of "natural boundaries," supported by the philosophy of natural law, was put forward to prove that the Rhine frontier was demanded by sovereign reason, if indeed it was not an eternal human truth. But as soon as that frontier created by bountiful Mother Nature had been reached, the revolutionary terminology of the Rhineland policy became superfluous. The application of pure force which took the French even beyond the natural frontiers now required a new justification. And it was easy enough for the Empire to borrow from its inexhaustible storehouse of dazzling slogans a new catchword for the occasion. This whole gamut of political theories for one and the same thing is also noteworthy because the same theories have been resurrected as occasion required even in our own day, by the descendants of those who first devised them. And among the gullible they still possess a certain currency as irrefragable truths. If the French, in the first stages of their revolution, endeavored to surround themselves with buffer states for the sake of their "security," these quite ephemeral creations soon turned out to be nothing but means of transition to annexation pure and simple. As soon as the conviction had gained ground that he who would hold the Rhine must also cross the Rhine, the need for "security" led to the pursuit of an ever-advancing frontier, and of a policy of conquest which on solemn occasions spoke of its civilizing mission, but otherwise was guided always by its military motives alone, knowing that a control over the heart of Germany meant control over the entire continent. This, as we all know, was the key to Napoleon's policy of hegemony, the sharpest weapon he had in his titanic struggle with England. So it happened that in an age which had just dreamed the dream of eternal peace, the struggle for the so-called "natural" boundaries threatened to unleash an eternal war. The same generation of Frenchmen who had just proclaimed to the world the native rights of man and the sovereignty of nations as the new political creed, now proceeded without any scruples to tear millions of Germans in the oldest *Kulturland* of German soil out of their own body politic and to educate them on the battlefields of Western Europe to become "future Frenchmen."

This foreign rule was broken down by an alliance of the German people and the rest of Europe in a struggle which was at once the cradle of German national consciousness and of Prussian compulsory military service. The Germans call this war the War of Liberation, because their liberation, their very liberty, was at stake. From this point of view the French historian Aulard is right in maintaining that the Germans carried on this struggle with the true spirit of the revolution and at the same time with the ideas of Kant on eternal peace. It remained for the hostile propaganda of the World War to invent the fiction that the campaigns of 1813 to 1815 belonged to a series of "invasions" of French soil by the Germans. And as we know, there were European statesmen who even after the restoration of peace in 1919 refused to revise their historical judgments.

For the Europe of 1815 there was no doubt as to who was the conqueror and who the liberator. And the outstanding question of the day was: How can we give the liberated German lands their most permanent guarantee against a recurrence of the catastrophe which had befallen them? Although the victors contented themselves with restoring eighteenth century conditions along the Franco-German frontier, and with organizing this frontier for more effective resistance by the projection of Prussia into this region and by the establishment of the German Confederation, yet this phase of the outcome of the war proved the hardest blow of all for the French. Even though far-sighted historians revealed to them the true causes of their downfall, the really active political minds of the generation which entered upon the period of peace after 1815 were not willing to renounce this part of the Napoleonic heritage.

Among all nations and at all times there have been individuals and groups of men who have aimed to extend the influence of their own state at the expense of other peoples. Noble and ignoble impulses always combine to set waves of chauvinism in motion, and history would be engaging in moral judgments, which is not its function, were it to make a whole nation accountable for the intentions of individuals. But here we are not considering individuals; we are considering rather the spirit of the nation. To be sure the masses engaged in the daily struggle for existence are essentially not bellicose, but peace-loving. But, the spirit of a nation must be judged by the type of men to whom it instinctively entrusts political leadership, and by the points of view which are habitually the decisive factors in questions of foreign policy. In France the old Monarchy and the Convention, the Directory and the Empire, all bequeathed to their adherents the living traditions of a Rhine policy; and for the history of France during the nineteenth century it is a decisive fact that the parties which, after the terrible experience of the Napoleonic era are found battling for leadership at home, can hardly be distinguished from one another in this one respect. Although differing perhaps by a shade in their motives, they all agree in their observance of an irresistible and binding tradition. This is the bond uniting all French parties—a tacit understanding which transcends all their animosities, so that in this point they fairly vie with each other when necessary in giving proof of their patriotism and of their right to the leadership of a great nation.

It was the vital will of the nation not to accept "the treaties of 1815" on this very sore point, and to discard them at a favorable moment. In doing so it was not possible to use as a serious argument the pretext of foreign oppression, that motive of "security" which so often proves dangerous for a neighbor. For, as every Frenchman knew, this German Confederation which was powerless to carry out any active foreign policy, let alone a successful offensive, was no greater a menace than the quiescent spirit of the Germans during the post-Napoleonic age. But even the German Confederation with its purely defensive character was an unwelcome neighbor according to the traditional political thought of the French, and the new position of Prussia on the Rhine, established particularly at the desire of England in order to make the western German frontier secure once more and thereby to promote the safety of all Europe, seemed unbearable to them. This condition was opposed to all their traditional convictions and proved a barrier to their dreams of hegemony. It was felt to be a symbol of French defeat. Immediately after 1815 royalists like Bonald and Chateaubriand agreed in this with liberals like Béranger and with old Napoleonists. The men of the July revolution, too, like A. Thiers, and even the radical and socialist opponents of the bourgeois monarchy, like L. Blanc, all struck the same note in this question. It echoed through the era of Napoleon III and was adhered to even after the defeat of 1870. Did not Clemenceau, one of the most steadfast guardians of such heritages, repeatedly utter the assurance that the *revanche* prepared during the time of the Third Republic, was not only for Sedan but also for Waterloo?

If the arrangements of 1815 were thus rejected as a whole, it was primarily the central stipulation, Prussia's Watch on the Rhine, which the passionate instinct of the nation sought to undo. At any rate political experience had taught that the road to this goal could be covered only by stages, only by indirect means, and only during a favorable situation in European politics. Even those who demanded the whole of the Rhine for France knew that they would have to bide their time. They spoke of Belgium, of parts of Holland, of Luxemburg, of the frontiers of 1814

(Saarbrücken, Saarlouis, Landau), and of the removal of the Prussian arms from the Rhine. In short, so far as the German left bank was concerned, they would have been content, for the time being, to restore its former military impotence. But no matter what the immediate objective was, every responsible French government knew that even if the idea of a Rhine frontier cautiously advanced could be realized, this would be possible only against the opposition of the new Europe once more restored to peace, and that first of all the overthrow of the new order would have to be awaited, or—this was the next step—a favorable opportunity would have to be utilized for bringing about such an overthrow.

The crisis in the Near East in 1828–1829 furnished the first occasion. As early as the summer of 1828 a memorial of Chateaubriand, the Romanticist, who was then minister in Rome, won high praise in the royal council from La Ferronays, the minister for foreign affairs, because it stressed a thought which at that time stirred the French diplomats quite as much as it did public opinion at large. "We want the Rhine frontier from Strassburg to Cologne," said Chateaubriand. "That is our just claim." Since Austria and England will never agree to concede the Rhine frontier in return for an alliance, France must seek an alliance with Russia, and offer the

Russians Constantinople, in order to gain the Rhine for herself. "That must sooner or later become the boundary of France, not only for the sake of her honor but also in the interest of her security." It should be noted that it was the men of the Restoration, brought back to their Fatherland by the victories of the allies, including the Prussians, who were now voicing their old program of conquest, even if they veiled it with a pretext of security. They spoke the language of men who had learned nothing and forgotten nothing. As soon as the crisis in the Near East offered the slightest possibility of a European disturbance, the French government took up these plans officially, though in a somewhat veiled form. In the autumn of 1829 the minister, the Duc de Polignac, submitted to King Charles X the plan for a Franco-Russian alliance which aimed at the attainment of the Rhine goal by means of a new grouping of the European states. While the Russians were offered the Balkans, France was to have as her immediate spoils Belgium and Landau, and as her indirect reward there was to be established a buffer state west of the Rhine under a Dutch prince, and another east of the Rhine under the King of Saxony. Another project made the Saxon King head of a buffer state west of the Rhine, with his capital at Aix-la-Chapelle. So far as the German Rhine is concerned, this was a more modest program than outright annexation; on the other hand, it involved the breaking down of all the safety barriers which Europe had erected between Alsace and the North Sea. The statesmen of the Restoration thought they were pursuing a realistic policy in offering Saxony and Holland to Prussia as compensation. The plan to establish the King of the Netherlands upon the throne of Constantinople is evidence of how far the leaders in Paris were prepared to go in their fantastic schemes for the sake of resuming the Napoleonic policies with respect to the Rhine, and of regaining by military tactics the old open door to Western Germany. This is the first memorable example of a policy which Napoleon III developed into a system in the "sixties." Although the proposals of Polignac arrived in St. Petersburg too late, yet they were not forgotten, and even in 1868 the old royalists, with warnings and threats, reminded the Emperor of what they, true to the traditions of French glory, would have been ready to do in their own day.

Nor did these hopes die during the time of the July Monarchy. On the contrary, in the separation of Belgium from Holland, whereby one of the protective barriers of the Congress of Vienna was torn down, they found new inspiration. For the liberal period of French politics it was axiomatic that the idea of the liberation of oppressed peoples should be applied first of all to those who, it was claimed, had been separated from France against their will. While Talleyrand during the Belgian embroglio sought to win England over to his cunning plans, which would have betrayed all of the Rhineland to France, and while a hotspur like Armand Carrel refused to make peace until the last Prussian soldier had departed from the left bank of the Rhine, those who pursued a more reasonable policy of reconciliation, like the jurist Lerminier, contented themselves with a French "protectorate over the German cities on the Rhine." The alternative, complete annexation or autonomy of the Rhineland, was kept open even now. Then in 1840, when another serious crisis in the Near East caused a collision of the European powers, the French urge for action, flaring up in passionate desire, again turned toward the Rhine. As minister, Thiers demanded a war for the European balance of power and aroused the press to a vociferous cry that France should go to war for the west bank of the Rhine. Even in poetry, the slogan of the journalists found inspiring echoes. Only those more peacefully inclined racked their brains to find some suitable compensation whereby they might make renunciation more tasteful to their obstinate neighbor. Even a man trained in German thought like the philosopher E. Quinet endeavored to prove to the Germans that the Rhine represented their past, the Danube their future.

Hence there is no denying the fact that though the views as to the best method, be it force or "conciliation," differed widely, there was agreement as to the objective, and every internal upheaval in France brought to the surface the same bubbles from the depths of this seething desire. If, on the other hand, we look at the German people during these decades, we find them entirely occupied with themselves,—peaceful not only so far as the masses but also the politically leading upper strata were concerned,—still making their first feeble attempt to regain a consciousness of its unity, and to determine its own political destinies. Who, then, was to blame that this awakening self-consciousness gradually took its light and leading from a spirit of opposition to a power which cherished such presumptuous desires and, as if the times had not changed, did not tire of demanding for itself the oldest German *Kulturland?* Even in the stormy year when the revolutionary urge for self-determination inscribed the watchwords of unity and liberty on the German banners, the new French leaders, in spite of the serious shock suffered by their own state, did not allow their lurking hopes to wane, and only the all-pervading national enthusiasm of the Germans of 1848 prevented them from laying hands upon the hot iron. Even such a man as Alexis de Tocqueville, whose name is free from suspicion of gross chauvinism, justified, in July, 1840, when he was minister of state, the arrest of some Palatinate republicans in Paris, by stating quite openly that these men belonged to the very party which had most strenuously opposed "the tendency of the French nation to extend its frontiers to the Rhine." And the Liberal A. Thiers is credited with the rash dictum that if he had had his own way in 1848 he would have extended the frontier of France as far as Mayence and thus have secured control of the keys to Germany. The herald of the Napoleonic legend was destined, even as a critic of the policies of Napoleon III, never to lose sight of this fleeting vision.

II

In this France, in this spirited and political atmosphere, Louis Napoleon rose to prominence, heir to a name which had been the very embodiment of those claims to the Rhine; surrounded by parties whose ambitions were, at favorable times, always buoyed up by this one great dream; taught from earliest childhood to ride roughshod over all the parties of his ambitious and excitable nation, and to commend himself to the soul of the nation as the true leader of promise.

The experience of the First Empire stood out before the eyes of this adventurer who possessed naught but his name. It burned within his breast and was a fillip to his will. But this brooder, whose every thought centered about this single idea, had carefully pondered the causes for the collapse of the First Empire and knew what he would have to avoid. Just as he believed in his mission, so too he was conscious of the inherent dangers of his task. He who depended for his future upon the name of Napoleon would have to avoid the excesses connected with this name. In harmony with the ideas of a new age, and with the help of forces which the great Napoleon had mistakenly allowed to contribute to his downfall, this lesser Napoleon planned a new ascent and a new Bonapartism, which was to take over the heritage of the First Empire. In his *Idées Napoléoniennes* he had sought to coin a modern ideology for this Bonapartism, continuing the process begun in the memoirs of St. Helena of pouring new wine into old bottles. Anyone who examines this manifesto of a pretender, will notice that every phrase is chosen with a definite objective in view and that it is genuine only as an expression of will, not as a formulation of thought. Although the nationalist impulses of the century are recognized it is not done for their own sake, but because through them the arrangements of the Congress of Vienna, the network of treaties of 1815 woven from the tatters of the empire, could be blown to pieces as with a charge of dynamite. Everything is in the service of that fixed idea which held the pretender in its grasp. And he knew how to make distinctions. Among these national impulses there were those of Italy, in the subterranean mazes of which Louis Napoleon had wandered even as a youth. The Italian aspirations, culminating in the establishment of national unity, met his unqualified approval. But when he spoke of the German national movement, he expressed himself much more cautiously. To be sure, he condemned the exaggerated demands of the First Empire, which had cast its eyes as far as Hamburg and Lübeck. On the other hand he was careful not to speak in the same tone of Cologne and Mainz, of Speyer and Aix-la-Chapelle. The Rhine he did not mention at all. He was shrewd enough to arouse no hopes which from the very outset would be likely to mobilize a new coalition of European powers against a pretender. Yet he was careful also not to destroy any hopes which were inseparably bound up with his name in France. Hence he was silent. Those who would read his inmost thoughts should study the following significant but ambiguous sentence: "The France of Henry IV, Louis XIV, Colbert and Napoleon has the mission of thrusting its sword of Brennus into all treaties, in the interest of civilization." Is that not the language of the First Empire?

This was Napoleon's guiding motive as he rose to power and faced the task of veiling his policy of ruthless might by deeds and successes and national fame. But this pensive observer, who so long had watched the European situation for chances to make his ascent, was clear on one point, namely that if he openly resumed the old classical Rhine policy of his predecessors, the great coalition before which his uncle had succumbed would be brought back to life. Besides, such a policy was hardly in keeping with his nature or his talents.

Only when the European horizon became so clouded that the members of the family of nations were again pitted against one another in hostile array, only during a great crisis, was it possible to hope for a bold realization of the French dreams or at least of a part of them. The policy of the Emperor in the Crimean War shattered for the first time the old concert of great powers. The next shock, the Italian war of 1859, was the first trial of a policy of allying with the national idea and thereby increasing the power of France and extending her frontiers. After the success of the action the problem was to repeat in Germany the game played with Cavour in Italy. It was a question of making moderate gains and at the same time satisfying the avid imagination of the people in its most sensitive aspect.

Since the political manifestoes of Napoleon were fond of proclaiming pompously their watchwords to Europe as if they were doctrines and had full claim to universal recognition, it was natural that the belief should arise that the Emperor was being inspired and led by these doctrines as such. And since he finally suffered defeat at the end of his adventuresome career, the conviction became general among the French that he failed merely because he had followed a doctrinaire and un-French policy of nationalities and had forgotten the great traditions of the classical French foreign policy, above all the Rhine policy. But in reality the Emperor was so far from abandoning this objective that he was ever concerned about new ways and means of reaching it in consonance with the prevailing circumstances. Throughout his entire life he brooded over the European map and remained on the alert to discover the right method of bringing about a situation in European politics favorable for his plans. This situation would have to culminate in a break between Prussia and Austria, followed by the dissolution of the unwelcome German Confederation. That was the prerequisite for all success, the first step on a road which was necessarily wrapped in obscurity and has even to this day remained somewhat concealed from posterity.

For setting the inactive mass of Europe in motion there was—paradoxical as it may sound—hardly a stronger ferment available than the national German movement for unification, which after the failure of its first efforts of 1848–1849 began to show signs of renewed activity at the end of the 'fifties. If Prussia took the lead in this (as Piedmont had done in the Italian movement), the German Powers were bound to clash again, until from their rivalry there would follow the dissolution of the Confederation and the advent of chaos, which would give the shrewd schemer—and here the seeming paradox is solved—the possibility of an easy pillaging expedition. Hence it was necessary for Napoleon first to commend himself to the Prussians as an admirer of a truly German policy for Prussia and as a benevolent and disinterested friend. That is the meaning of the confidential conversation which he had in April, 1857, at Paris with Bismarck, Prussia's coming man. As we know, Bismarck relates it on more than one occasion, and in his *Gedanken und Erinnerungen* (Thoughts and Recollections) he describes it as the opening wedge in this Napoleonic campaign. On that occasion the Emperor developed his idea of a grandiose rounding-out of Prussia in North Germany, but at the same time he took pains to emphasize his own disinterestedness and to disavow all plans of conquest along the Rhine, because even if they succeeded temporarily they would in the end lead only to the formation of European coalitions and would thus be doomed to failure. Although now and then there was a suggestion of a modest rectification of boundaries, yet the plan was so laid that not a spark of distrust should be aroused in the opponent's breast. The real motive was not the alleged desire for the naval strengthening of a Prussianized North Germany to act as a counterbalance to England; it was rather the well considered plan to instil in Prussia new hope and ambition after a period of renunciation, and to make the "German question" an element of high politics.

Not until the new era had begun in Prussia and a new alignment of forces had followed the Italian war, did this possibility actually loom up. Now there were heard in Paris and Berlin gentle hints on the part of the Emperor about desirable cooperation and a possible slight rectification of boundaries. What lay concealed in the inmost recesses of his heart, however, was not revealed to the Prussians. But the Emperor did reveal his real intentions in April, 1860, to his minister in Berlin, Marquis Moustier. The Belgian minister Baron Beyens has recently uncovered this source. Napoleon prefaced his train of thought with the statement that the economic advantage of England over France rested upon the secure geographical position of the former, while France, being exposed to attacks on several sides, was forced to resort to expensive measures of security. For that reason France would have to arrive at a system of boundaries which would serve as a defence *per se*. Nice and Savoy covered the Italian flank, and the neutrality of Belgium prevented an attack from the north. But on the line from Mainz to Cologne, he went on to say, boundary rectifications were absolutely necessary. In other words, he said, he had in mind the Palatinate and the left bank of the Rhine. "However, I am not dreaming of conquests, I wish to advance peacefully and gradually; I desire to reach my goal by friendly discussion and by understandings." [1] However far these suggestions, with

[1] Baron Beyens, *Le second Empire, vu par un diplomate belge* (Lille-Bruges. Paris, 1924). Vol. 1, p. 313: "Mais je ne rêve pas de conquêtes; je veux agir pacifiquement et progressivement; je veux arriver à mon but par un échange d'explications amiables et par des ententes."

their perspective of a rounding cut of Prussia in North Germany, may have been advanced at that time in Berlin—the manly words of King William erected a firm barrier against the tempter, and the spirit of public opinion, now grown watchful, kept a sharp eye upon the man who in an address from the throne had mentioned among other things the dangerous, two-faced watchword of the natural boundaries of France.

None the less the game went on, as is shown by the pamphlet "Le Rhin et la Vistule" (October, 1861), one of those semi-official publications which like seagulls announce the coming storm and which introduce, accompany and open for discussion the veiled policies of the Emperor. It had the double purpose of quieting German public opinion with regard to the Rhine frontier and at the same time of stopping up this source of unrest by a modest amicable proposal. The protest which it contained was directed against the boundary of 1815, "which has systematically opened to the enemy our valleys of Lorraine and our plains of Champagne, and which has broken the line of our frontier, in order to tear away from France the cities fortified by us, like Landau, and those built by us, like Saarlouis." In other words, restoration of the boundary of 1814, which France needed for her defence. "Without irritating the national pride of

Germany, it would satisfy our inborn passion for the Rhine, and at the same time the most recent fears of the Germanic populations. This line, based on mutual agreement, would be final, and the dream which is dear to so many on this side of the Rhine but rests like a nightmare on Germany and Belgium, would vanish forever." In such sentimental tones the stubborn German was shown that he would have to appease the Gallic dreams and ambitions which were directed at the *grand Rhin,* by conceding the *petit Rhin*—"forever." The English minister Lord Clarendon was quite right when he warned the Queen of the fixed idea of Napoleon that he could secure his dynasty only by the territorial aggrandizement of France. For the moment, he said, only the honesty of King William had frustrated such plans, but the Emperor might at any time be expected to seize the left bank of the Rhine. And he added that the whole population of France, regardless of party affiliations, would be delighted if he did so. From the English point of view the minister advised the Queen to arm and to issue a warning to the people against a hostile attack (October 20, 1861). That was the opinion of King William too. He yielded neither to intimidation nor to compromise.

And so Napoleon's hopes began to rise again only when, at the end of the new era, that statesman assumed the leadership in Prussian politics whose courage and unscrupulousness he trusted would make him a Prussian Cavour and who, he hoped, would not be too ethical to accept a modest broker's fee. Naturally the disappointment was great when the new minister, whose mind he had tried so hard to read in 1862, did not after all pursue the course which the Napoleonic schemer had expected. For in gambling away the sympathies of Germany by intensifying the domestic conflict, it seemed that Bismarck would be able to follow only an old-fashioned Prussian policy, instead of embarking upon the nationalist activities which had been expected of him. And when during the Polish uprising he allied himself closely with Russia by means of the Alvensleben Convention (February, 1863), it seemed fully proved that he could never be expected to break with the traditional Prussian policy or show himself susceptible to the alluring suggestions from Paris. And so the emperor, seeing all his previous speculations frustrated, suddenly switched over to the other side.

If the great movement could not be brought about through Prussia and a German national policy, it would have to be started from the opposite side. Accordingly Napoleon decided to approach his definite objective with the help of Austria and in conjunction with the Polish national struggle.

On February 21, 1863, he offered to the Austrian ambassador, at first through the Empress Eugenie, who was used in such cases as the seductive advance guard, then on February 24 in personal negotiations, an alliance which aimed at a radical revision of the map of Europe.[1] Even the plan of Polignac of 1829, which had similar aims to be attained through an alliance with Russia, was harmless as compared with the grandiose barter into which Austria was to be coaxed. And the well-known plan for partitioning the Turkish Empire, which the Tsar Nicholas suggested to the English ambassador in 1853, would have been no menace at all to the peace of Europe, in comparison with this project. The upheaval which Napoleon planned would have led to nothing short of world war. The point of departure was to be the resurrection of Poland, directed against Russia and Prussia, just as previously the Italian national struggle had been exploited against Austria. But the objective was the acquisition of the left bank of the Rhine. While there were losses as well as gains involved for

[1] The documents upon which the following account is based are published in the original German work of Hermann Oncken, *Die Rheinpolitik Kaiser Napoleons III. von 1863–1870 und der Ursprung des Krieges von 1870–71,* 3 vols., Stuttgart, Berlin and Leipzig, 1926. The present translation limits itself to Professor Oncken's "Darstellung" (Vol. 1, pp. 1–120). Only a few of the most important documents are quoted in the Appendix.—Translator's note.

all the others, France was only to gain. To be sure, a system of adjustments was to be devised to satisfy all. Austria for example was to be compensated for the loss of Venetia and Galicia by Bosnia, Serbia, Silesia and South Germany. But was it reasonable to expect that Russia could be persuaded to give up her part of Poland by a promise of Asiatic Turkey, or that Prussia would acquiesce in the loss of Silesia, Posen and the left bank of the Rhine in return for the magnanimous offer of a boundary rectification in the north? Such a project could be realized only by the terrible catastrophes of war. But the vision of the future: Italy free to the Adriatic, Poland restored, the Rhine a French river [1]—such was Eugenie's interpretation of the plans—signified a European system in which the preponderance of France would have supplanted the previous balance of power, as it had done before only in the heyday of French glory. The reader is referred to Metternich's reports: the Empress quivering with emotion, feverish with impatience, all "fire and flame," her notes as persuasive as those of a woman in love, promising everything and demanding everything, and intent upon using the golden opportunity for the *furia francese*, as she says. And behind her the Emperor himself, so consumed by political passion that his

[1] See Note 1 in the Appendix.

wonted taciturnity is broken by "immeasurable ambition and uncontrollable energy." The ambassador was reminded of the Emperor's language prior to the great epoch of the Crimean War and the War of 1859. At the peak of his power and still undismayed by defeat, Napoleon believed that he could launch this ruthless venture against the peace of the world. On the other hand, compare with this the responsible peace policy of Bismarck at the time of Germany's greatest power. Never had the soul of the imperial adventurer been laid so bare, and it would indeed have been his most brilliant coup to realize his plans on the Polish side at the expense of the German nation in the east and west and to set fire to the world for the sake of the Rhine.

But Austria refused, and even after many years Napoleon and Eugenie still continued to reproach Metternich with this sin. Since England too sensed the desire for the Rhine behind the Polish action and withdrew in suspicion when the Polish uprising was crushed by the Russians, the whole plan collapsed and Napoleon hastily resumed his former policies. As early as April, 1863, his minister Drouyn de Lhuys made the official declaration to the Prussian ambassador that from the very beginning of the Polish crisis the Paris government had had no ulterior motives and had planned no disturbance of its relations to Prussia. He added that the truth of his declaration was vouched for by the fact that he was making it unsolicited, since he would not utter a lie unless obliged to do so. As a matter of fact, Napoleon had every reason to dispel all distrust which might have arisen in Berlin, for now he planned once more to set in motion through Prusso-German channels the machinery which he had failed to move through Poland and Austria.

Once more the Prussians were showered with signs of the imperial confidence. On June 8, 1863, Napoleon disclosed to the Prussian diplomat Prince Reuss what he himself considered a correct policy for Prussia. He, the Emperor, instead of steering into the conflict on the military question, as King William had done, would have proclaimed to his country the words of Ernst Moritz Arndt: "My fatherland must be larger" (these words the good Emperor quoted in German) and the program: "Give me a strong army and I will give you a strong fatherland." To be sure, he said, the treaties of 1815 were in the way, but that could be arranged. A striking paradox this: a Napoleon reminding the Hohenzollerns, to the strains of a German patriotic song, of Prussia's mission! Can it be true after all that he was the inveterate doctrinaire that many French critics make him out to be? In reality he never lost sight of his goal. After the Polish lever had proved impracticable, he was forced to furnish the Prussian ambitions with an incentive, especially in the period of the assembly of the princes at Frankfurt (Fürstentag) when an agreement between Austria and Prussia would have meant a firm barrier against all dreams of conquest. But Bismarck's infallible acumen asserted itself. His marginal comment on Napoleon's remark that all this could be arranged was the following cool question: "By the cession of the Rhine?" With these words he reached the very heart of the matter.

This episode, like the former, remained a mere episode. One proposal is followed by another, but all of them reveal the fact that their author is a politician who knows what he wants. Indeed, his will sees nothing so clearly as his final objective, and this series of little preludes is instructive for the very reason that it reveals the constancy of Napoleon's goal, however wavering his methods may have been. From this point of view alone his policies of the next few years can be understood.

The European crisis which he tried to force in one way or another soon presented itself automatically by the death of King Frederick VII of Denmark (November, 1863) and by the reopening of the Schleswig-Holstein question. Fate threw into his lap the chance which he craved—provided the program of strengthening Prussia in North Germany, and Prussia's embarkation upon an expansive policy of German nationalism could be realized through this crisis.

To be sure the policy which Bismarck adopted in the Schleswig-Holstein question was open to grave criticism from the French point of view. In the first place the French objected to Prussia's cooperation with Austria, which postponed indefinitely the break on which everything depended; then Prussia restricted herself to the "petty, miserable" Schleswig-Holstein question, instead of attacking the "large" question at once and proclaiming a German program of action which would have hastened the break. So long as war had not actually begun, Napoleon had to restrain himself all the more. When Bismarck late in December, 1863, had trapped the Emperor's minister General Fleury into betraying the cue by mentioning the Rhineland, and the General reported to Paris that the word had been mentioned, a telegram came back from Napoleon with the anxious instruction: "Do not speak of the Rhine." At no cost was Berlin to be allowed to become suspicious, since only a short time before the Emperor had committed himself so damagingly with regard to Austria. So long as the action had not yet been begun, he could afford to have his alliance seen from a distance, but his own bill of conpensations had to be guarded most cautiously. Only after the outbreak of the war had created an accomplished fact and England seemed inclined to help Denmark, while the good will of France appeared to have risen in price, even with respect to Berlin, did Paris dare to use clearer language. As soon as the Prusso-Austrian troops had crossed the frontier of Jutland, the French minister for foreign affairs deemed it appropriate, in an interview with the Prussian ambassador, to speak in favor of the annexation of Schleswig-Holstein "and some of the adjacent territory" and also to indicate unequivocally the trend of his own appetite, namely for the boundaries of 1814 and for an autonomous Rhenish state according to the model of Belgium.[2] For the first time a counter-claim was officially though not bindingly mentioned—a minimum claim which could if necessary be made to square with Napoleon's principle of nationalities, since it did not actually aim at annexation. The only question was whether the Prussians would under such conditions renew the game which Napoleon had played with Cavour at Plombières. When the Prussian ambassador turned a deaf ear and no reaction at all came

[2] See Note 2 in the Appendix. All similar references below refer also to the Appendix.

from Berlin, the opinion gained ground in Paris that it would be best to hasten the Prussian resolution with gentle threats, especially since public opinion was constantly becoming more restive over the incursion into Jutland. With repeated references to the larger field of endeavor open for Germany, the possible alternatives were indicated. They were either an alliance on the basis of a system of annexations and compensations acceptable to Prussia, or war. But the threat, like the lure, missed its mark. Napoleon was bound to realize that if he became still more insistent he could merely commit Bismarck more strongly to Austria and force him to extreme moderation in the Schleswig-Holstein question. There was nothing to do but wait, else a premature uncovering of his cards would spoil the whole game and altogether drive his stout-hearted opponent, who held all his trumps firmly in his hand, into the camp of the enemy. It was his hope that the Schleswig-Holstein affair would ultimately, without his interference, lead to serious tension between Prussia and Austria, and that thereby he would be offered an opportunity to initiate his own political action.

This possibility arose for the first time when in the summer of 1865 an open outbreak of the conflict between the two great German powers seemed inevitable. This time Napoleon was careful to refrain from disquieting the Prussians by untimely hints of compensation, so as not to diminish the chances for an outbreak of war. Although the Italian premier La Marmora replied to Bismarck's soundings with regard for an alliance that by a sacrifice in the Rhine province Prussia could make the outcome of the conflict certain, Paris itself showed an air of renunciation. To the question of the Prussian ambassador the Empress Eugenie replied that France had no demands and desired only to remain at peace (August 11, 1865). Drouyn de Lhuys was willing to go so far as to bind himself, in the case of an understanding with Prussia, to claim "no rectification of the Prussian boundary" (August 20, 1865), which to be sure would not have excluded a rectification *along* the *German* frontier.

We can imagine the unpleasant surprise of Napoleon when in spite of his well considered renunciation the will to peace conquered over the plans for war at Berlin. That through the Convention of Gastein (August 14, 1865) Austria and Prussia again patched up their troubles was felt as a personal affront at Paris. French public opinion raged because the hope of a German civil war, which seemed so close at hand, had suddenly vanished. And in an official proclamation Drouyn de Lhuys utterly condemned this convention in the name of the popular conscience. Bismarck knew well where to seek the root of this sudden change of heart: "I could have won the Rhine frontier if the two great powers had not been so ignoble as to come to an understanding for the time being."

But since Napoleon soon strove to erase these gross impressions and again began to whisper in the ear of the ambassador, Count Goltz, that Prussia should assume the leadership in Germany, the Prussian premier felt that the time had come for having a personal interview with the Emperor and sounding out his ultimate aims. His journey to Biarritz (October, 1865), early set into a false light by prejudiced persons, soon became the subject of exaggerated stories which told of offers made by Bismarck and even of agreements. In reality the soundings of both sides never got beyond the first stages. To be sure, Bismarck had come with the fear that definite proposals would be made to him which he might be unable to recommend to his king. But since Drouyn de Lhuys in Paris had expressly renounced any desire to acquire Prusso-German territory, he too made no proffers, but declared that developments would have to be awaited. The same attitude was assumed also by Napoleon in Biarritz when he decided not to force matters but to allow them to mature. And although Bismarck did not withhold the hope that Schleswig-

Holstein would be but the first step in an active German policy on the part of Prussia, the emperor was very careful, after his previous experiences, not to voice any desires or plans of his own. For he was convinced that the other party was bound to come to him in time and that until then silence was golden. If the French press now created the impression that France had listened very passively to many proposals from Bismarck, this was done solely for the purpose of strengthening the Austrians in their controversy with Prussia and of obviating the unpleasant possibility of another compromise between the two German powers.

France was keeping under cover, silent and inscrutable, so as not to disturb the gradual trend toward war.

III

WHEN in February, 1866, the break between Austria and Prussia became imminent, the hour which Napoleon longed for had arrived. His dreams began to assume real form, for at last they had reached the stage of practical politics. But a shrewd ruse patiently executed was still necessary in order to make sure that the break between the German powers should lead to war. Since Austria as well as Prussia looked to Paris for the final decision, Napoleon was faced by the task of making the decision to go to war easier for both sides. Of course a different method had to be used with each. He had to ease their minds with regard to his own attitude and the conditions of his own friendship, and at the same time, without prejudicing the chances of war, he had to make sure of his own gains in German territory if possible through written agreements with each of the two rivals.

The character of such a policy, which plays different tunes on different instruments, is bound to be obscure, and not before we are in a position to combine all its expressions and acts and to illuminate them by constant comparison, can we get a clearer picture of it and of the secret motives which lay behind it. It would be a vain attempt to try, by means of the ministerial documents of the *Origines diplomatiques de la guerre de 1870–71*, to get at the bottom of a complicated policy whose final direction lay in the hands of the Emperor alone. Such an analysis would hardly get beyond the outward preliminaries of the diplomatic events. It is essential for our purpose to hear Napoleon himself talking now in one vein to the Austrian ambassador, and now in another to the Prussian, and now in still another to the representatives of the Middle States. In this way alone we can deduce the logical course of his policy, making a synthesis of his methods, hints, retractions, encouragements and discouragements and groping our way through the maze of ambiguities which even at that time furnished endless riddles to those who looked on.

As befits a mighty monarch, Napoleon was constantly talking of peace, but with the hope always uppermost in his mind that war would not slip away from him this time. He was ever harping upon his strict neutrality, so that none of the parties would become suspicious of him and abandon all thoughts of war; and yet this benevolent impartiality was designed to throw so much weight into the one balance or the other that this skilful distribution of influence always made for the inevitability of war. But the greatest skill was required in gradually making known, in small doses, the plans which he secretly cherished of strengthening and enlarging France. The experience of the last years had taught that the party with the stronger will for action should not be frightened by premature demands for compensation. There was more wisdom in encouraging it by friendly words, so that it would proceed steadfastly. Above all the alliance with Italy (April 8, 1866), though not formally facilitated was consciously sanctioned, this being the prerequisite for any action by Berlin. By doing so Napoleon sacrificed an important card, to be sure. But in order to strengthen the cautious will to war in the opposing camp as well, the central states were given to understand that they should take sides, rather than observe a sickly neutrality, and this meant of course to take the side of Austria. For French policy, desiring to play a decisive rôle in the creation of the new German state, was interested not in a localized duel between the two great powers, but rather in an all-embracing German civil war. But as soon as Austria became perturbed by the reports of an imminent Prusso-Italian alliance, the time was ripe for the exertion of a slight pressure on the part of Paris. Austria was given to understand that the first absolute prerequisite would be the surrender of Venetia to Italy, in return for adequate compensation, of course. And when such compensation in the Near East was indignantly rejected by Austria, the German territory of Silesia was suggested. Thereby the Austrian will to war was stimulated by being given a worthy objective, and a shrewdly devised chain of compensations was forged, the last links of which lay at the very source of the whole Napoleonic policy—at the Rhine.

To the lay observer who comprehended only parts of this deceitful game it must have seemed at times as if the one hand were ignorant of what the other was doing. But actually both were guided by the ardent desire of bringing on war and of making the war an occasion for pillage. This game was made easier for the Emperor, but at times too more difficult, by the fact that opposing tendencies held sway at court, in the government, and among the people. The Empress Eugenie, the foreign minister Drouyn de Lhuys, and in the camp of the opposition A. Thiers, who in 1840 and 1848 had already dreamed of an advance to the Rhine, all cherished the ideas of the classical Rhine policy and hence favored the Austrian side. On May 3, at the very height of the crisis, Thiers in a brilliant address before the legislature, showed profound distrust of any German national movement and championed the traditional methods of the French foreign policy, the program of a Germany composed of independent states, which, as he said, had been a French axiom and a European principle ever since the peace of Westphalia. On the other side Prince Napoleon and the friends of Italy, the Republicans, expressed themselves unequivocally in favor of Italy and indirectly for Prussia. And since they were more friendly to the idea of nationalism, they realized that no progress at all could be made in Germany unless this idea were encouraged. By this process to be sure, they hoped to get quite as much for France as their opponents.

But the Emperor, who alone had a general view of the situation, allowed both parties freedom of action to a certain extent, exploited them whenever he chose, and combined them in a sort of larger and more effective unit.

Drouyn de Lhuys later admitted that it had been the basic motive of the Emperor to conclude similar treaties with Austria and Prussia prior to the outbreak of war, and that these treaties were to have assigned the Rhine to France in return for neutrality.[3] That hits the nail on the head, but it does not adequately describe the difficulty of concluding both treaties at the same time, each different from the other in detail, without jeopardizing the basic purpose of the whole scheme, namely the outbreak of war.

We know that Napoleon's program contained several practical alternative possibilities, all of them serving as steps toward one final goal. In the foreground was the idea of a Rhenish buffer state. Even in the days of the Restoration and the Bourgeois monarchy this idea had been under consideration and served, now as then, as a minimum demand. It had the advantage of avoiding complete annexation and an outright challenge to the nationalist sentiment in Germany. It could even be brought into harmony with the ideology of the imperial policy of nationality. At any rate the plan called for the complete separation of such a buffer state (*état tampon*) from the German Confederation, the establishment of an autonomous neutral German Rhenish state, although at times there was vague talk of the possibility of merely separating such a state from Prussia and allowing it to remain in the Confederation. All these ambiguous projects aimed ultimately at the artificial creation of a second Belgium and represented a new step in the policy of surrounding France on her eastern frontier with a belt of dependent creations which would not only satisfy all the requirements of "security" but also animate the hope of future "penetration."

These prospects supplied the motives underlying the plans for an autonomous Rhenish state. In a session of the Council of Minister and the Council of State on May 18, 1866, the Duc de Persigny, the old confidant of the Emperor, whose voice was still listened to, supported a program which drew a fantastic picture of the functions of this Rhenish state, in consonance with the system of border states and "natural frontiers" devised during the Revolution. He said that the railways, the customs and the commercial relations could be skilfully used to prepare the way for a community of interests between the new state and the northeastern departments of

France; that the high French clergy could influence the Catholic population of the Rhineland; that the old historical memories could be aroused to form a Gallic Confederation embracing Holland, Belgium, Luxemburg, the Rhenish states and France, thus restoring the First Empire in all its glory, with the only difference that there would be princes instead of prefects at Brussels, The Hague, Mainz and Coblenz.[4] So much is known of this plan. According to the narrative of the duke himself the Emperor congratulated him confidentially the next day on his solution, saying that it was the natural and perhaps only way of "resuming" the Rhine frontier in future.

Now it was obvious that such aims could be made palatable to the Austrians more easily than to the Prussians. Already on April 29 Drouyn de Lhuys had submitted to the Austrian ambassador the following apparently harmless formula: If the war should add to the offensive strength of Germany, either under Austrian or Prussian leadership, France would desire a "neutralization" of the Rhineland under a neutral dynasty even a German one, with the proviso that both France and Germany should be bound not to infringe this neutrality.[5] This formula, which met no opposition on the part of Austria, was tacitly made the basis of the negotiations leading to the conclusion of the treaty of

June 12. Of course it was more difficult to come to an understanding on such a project with Prussia, which was directly affected territorially and would have violated its own policy of nationalism if it had acceded. Since even the most cautious and devious feelers brought no answer, the French finally refrained from even mentioning the *grand Rhin*, fearing to unnerve Prussia by any demands at all. But the ultimate objective was not abandoned and the hope was cherished that by means of a far-reaching system of adjustments and annexations Prussia would finally be prevailed upon to make the painful sacrifice.

It was easier perhaps to talk with Prussia about the *petit Rhin*. This meant at least the boundaries of 1814 (Saarbrücken, Landau), to which Napoleon had recurred again and again since the beginning of the 'sixties. But to the French mind this frontier rectification seemed so slight that it required a complement in the shape of the Bavarian Palatinate and adjacent territory. But the farther such a claim went, the more it smacked of annexation and had to be concealed from the Middle States. And when Prussia was sounded with regard to a possible acquisition of non-Prussian territory, Bismarck evaded the suggestion with the clever reply that his policy of drawing Bavaria over as much as possible to the Prussian side would not permit the assumption of such an obligation. This convinced the French of the necessity of an understanding between Bavaria and Austria. In other words, the expansion of the *petit Rhin* program was still confronted by internal obstacles. But if it could be expanded, say so as to include the Moselle boundary, it would assure the French of a genuine gain, just as important as that which the more indefinite *grand Rhin* promised. And if the two could be combined, the most ambitious French hopes would be realized.

It was natural that as soon as the diplomatic action of Napoleon began, the various methods which he employed had to come into play quite independently of one another. At the same time that he opened negotiations with the Austrians, speaking of Venetia, a neutral Rhenish state and a Silesian compensation, the Emperor informed the Prussians that although he was well disposed toward them, Austria had already made definite proposals to him and the eyes of the whole French nation were focused on the Rhine. A few days later he couched his thought in the following terms: In case Prussia should be enlarged, everyone could demand *quelque chose du côté de Rhin, vers la Moselle et du côté de la Bavière rhénane* (something along the Rhine, toward the Moselle and in Rhenish Bavaria). The policy of playing off one side against the other had begun, and with intense interest Paris and all of France looked on without fully understanding, while the Emperor held the scales and helped to excite the avidity of public opinion by his impenetrable attitude, dictated by the situation.

The first attempt proved unsuccessful. Although the Austrian ambassador was instructed on May 5 to consent to the surrender of Venetia and tacitly to approve of the sacrifice of the Rhineland, in case the neutrality of France and Italy could thus be secured, Napoleon's attempt to get a similar guarantee from Italy and to draw the latter from the side of the ally which he had only just found for her, met with failure. Austria withdrew, and the negotiations were held up. Since Napoleon now began to fear that Austria might be driven to a reconciliation with the Prussians, while the latter had witnessed a rebirth of the French ambitions along the Rhine, he took pains, on May 7, to renounce in the presence of the Prussian ambassador, all these ambitions, saying that he desired absolutely nothing. By this sudden renunciation he hoped to revive the aggressive spirit of the Prussians, which he feared had waned.

Meanwhile he was preparing a new form of diplomatic pressure in order to keep the crisis from ebbing. He proposed the idea of a European congress, which was to settle the Venetian and Schleswig-Holstein problems and adjust the whole German question. Although he described this as a new offer of peace, he was well aware that it would involve for Austria the unreasonable demand that she consent to allow a European areopagus to decide the ownership of a province which was Austria's legal possession; on the other hand Prussia would be confronted by the necessity of abandoning all her ambitious plans, while at the same time the alliance with Italy would expire. But Napoleon believed that for these very reasons he could count upon a greater readiness of both parties to enter into negotiations.

But even this plan of drawing Bismarck out by means of a conference failed to achieve its purpose. All attempts made through unofficial Italian channels, behind the backs of Bismarck and Goltz, to approach King William or to press the French aims even in their mildest form (the establishment of new federated German states along the Rhine), were unsuccessful, even though King Victor Emmanuel, who was chiefly interested in conducting the war under the most favorable auspices, pleaded the absolute necessity of complying with the emperor's wishes. In spite of many hints Bismarck did not make the voluntary offers that Paris desired. He persisted in forcing the French Emperor to formulate his demands. Yet the latter in turn did not venture to do so officially, fearing that this would lead to a pacific compromise between Bismarck, or the King, and Austria. As a matter of fact Bismarck actually did seek, through the Gablentz mission, to open the road to a reconciliation with Vienna.

This situation was not altered when Napoleon, after his agreement with Russia and England, actually issued, on May 24, the invitations to the congress in the interest of peace. Although this congress was sure to interfere gravely with his own sovereign game, Bismarck even now refused to be dislodged from his position. He continued to make bold speeches about his own open-mindedness in such matters to Benedetti and the Italian general Govone, who begged him to whisper a few words into the Emperor's ear. But he refrained from binding himself, except that he diverted the discussion from the German linguistic territory to the French linguistic territory. Above all he kept open a line of retreat by reserving the decision for the King himself. Tentatively he accepted the congress and kept cool, sensing the tight position of his shrewd adversary, to whose inscrutability he opposed a fitting measure of indecision.

In this situation the Italian party in Paris, concerned over a possible complete defection of the Emperor to the Austrian side, made a last attempt to influence the stubborn Prussian antagonist. It was in the days when private politics still played into the actions of the great, when everyone was talking of shrewd "deals," and the Duc de Persigny was discussing them with almost anyone on the street who cared to listen. Under instructions from Prince Napoleon, who like the Empress was sometimes used as an advance guard, though against Prussia, the Hungarian emigré Colonel Kiss went to Berlin on May 30 with entirely novel proposals. Instead of French neutrality, a French alliance was now offered, but since this would in all probability have decided the war militarily, it was made to depend upon very decisive counter-claims. As compensation for France the proposed alliance provided for the boundaries of 1814, the Rhenish Palatinate and Rhenish Hessia, and the adjacent Prussian territory with its enclaves—in short the Moselle line, though exclusive of Mainz and Coblenz.[6] It would have been an imitation of the alliance between Napoleon and Cavour, only that the German equivalent for Nice and Savoy would have comprised a section with not less than one and one-third millions of purely German population. It should be noted that it was the "friends of Prussia" in Paris who in the eleventh hour volunteered the alliance, taking careful consideration of the Prussian sensibilities. But Bismarck refused even to talk to the king about this unofficial feeler. He continued to reassure his opponent with ambiguous phrases, but he was determined to continue his course without assuming any contractual obligation with regard to France. He was convinced that a German Cavour, who betrayed German territory to such an extent would be utterly impossible.

Now immediately after the last semi-official agent had returned with empty hands, the disappointed Emperor proceeded to come to an understanding with Austria which, more and more tortured by anxiety concerning Napoleon's real intentions, was now finally prepared for greater sacrifices in order to avoid the congress and determined to wage the war for German hegemony (the offers of the Gablentz mission had just been rejected). Thus the refusal of Austria to take part in the congress became the means which Napoleon had hoped for to carry out his Machiavellian scheme. In a memorable interview of June 3 he unburdened himself to Prince Metternich, in order to extend his hand to the weakening partner. He admitted frankly that he had flirted a little with Prussia (*j'ai eu des coquetteries pour la Prusse*), shown a certain consideration for the King and been favorably disposed to the latter's *petites ambitions*. "But that is not all," he said. "I tolerated the attitude of Prussia because I said to myself that when the moment comes to arrive at an understanding with me, the Prussians will build me a golden bridge. The Rhine provinces in the distance made my decision uncertain for a long time.[7] Now I have abandoned ideas of this kind, and having made this sacrifice, I say to myself today that I can gain only by an understanding with Austria." That the sacrifice had reference only to an agreement with Prussia and not to what he had planned to gain thereby, was revealed by the agreement with Austria, which was reached on June 12 on the basis of the compensation already stipulated on April 29. The obligations of Austria in Italy were made very clear. Austria promised to cede Venetia in case of a victory in Germany, and not to interfere with the new order in Italy even in case of a victory in the Peninsula. The German territorial revisions were left somewhat vaguer. They were to be arranged jointly by the two powers, France binding herself to recognize all territorial gains made by Austria, provided that they would not disturb the European equilibrium by establishing Austrian hegemony over all Germany. The concealed meaning of this agreement is revealed by the fact that in concluding it the Austrian ministers made a verbal declaration that they would not protest against a territorial modification which, enlarging Saxony, Württemberg and even Bavaria, would transform the Rhine Provinces into a new independent state.[8] Thus Austria paid for French neutrality alone the heavy price for which it had previously, early in May, wished to purchase Italian neutrality as well. A few days before Prussia destroyed the German Confederation by seceding, the foremost power in this Confederation, driven more and more to the wall by the intrigues of Napoleon to be sure, had deliberately abandoned the Rhine and renounced its German mission in the hour of decision, though, being ashamed of its own act, it voiced this renunciation only in a veiled verbal form.

If, then, Napoleon contractually secured his speculative gain on one side only and was unable to obtain a similar promise on the other, he was comforted by the fact that Prussia would be made more compliant by the expected outcome of the war. Moreover the Emperor had another card in reserve, which might for the present seem unimportant but might become a valuable trump in his hands. We refer to the German middle states. For months the Emperor did all in his power to convince them of French unselfishness and yet to involve them by all means in the coming crisis. Most instructive is the method employed in the treatment of Bavaria, which by virtue of situation and size seemed to have a freer hand than any of its associates and consequently to cherish special aspirations, although in reality its possession of the Palatinate exposed it so much the more to French aggression and more closely circumscribed its policy. Hence tempting proposals as well as threats were in order.

It was no wonder then that from the beginning of May until July the Bavarian minister in Paris was constantly being approached with strange allusions, for example with the observation that the military armaments in the Palatinate were causing France uneasiness. As if the five thousand men stationed there could have been a source of anxiety to the Empire! The object of these steps was not alone the reduction of the military force in a frontier province which, as we know, was involved in the future plans of France, but also the desire to let the leading middle state, which did not conceal its German sentiments, feel a gentle pressure which would in good season render it more pliable to the will of its powerful neighbor. But this neighbor had also an offer to make. As soon as the first skirmishes of the Bohemian campaign brought the Prussians victory after victory, Paris changed its tone altogether. On June 30 Drouyn de Lhuys in a confidential interview disclosed his personal opinion to the Bavarian minister.

It would be best, he said, if "those middle states and smaller states which really formed the heart of Germany," with Bavaria at their head, should form a confederation excluding Prussia and Austria, both of which had from the beginning used the confederation only for their own selfish interests and had maltreated their confederates. This group, he added, which could not possibly desire the perpetuation of the former confederation, enjoys the sympathy of the French. Behind the Parisian duplicity, which turned now to Prussia and now to Austria, there was a third theme, namely the old slogan of a third Germany, whose leadership France, with magnanimous impartiality, was prepared to assume. The outlines of the old *Rheinbund* program, in which the old French theories of the liberty of the German estates had once reached their culmination, were beginning to reappear.

And so the cards were shuffled for a game which, however well disguised it seemed, actually enlisted in its service all the traditions of French history. An expression of these various devices is found in the open letter of the Emperor to Drouyn de Lhuys of June 11, prior to the outbreak of the war, wherein he formulated his German program as follows: a closer relation between the middle states, strengthening and rounding off of Prussia in North Germany, and maintenance of Austria's strong position in Germany. What France demanded for herself in such a satisfactory (but impossible) squaring of the circle was suggested in the obscure statement that she desired no territorial increase—except in case the European balance should be disturbed and the neighboring provinces, by voluntary choice, should wish to be annexed to France. However shrewdly the network was woven—naturally even Napoleon's hand quivered and hesitated at times in the execution—every weakness was bound to become a source of strength when in the course of the war the hour for an arbitrator should arrive who, weapons in hand, might interpret these obscure statements.

Thus Napoleon III appears as a true representative of that traditional policy which since the seventeenth century had become an immutable component of the French (national) will to power. The impulse of the classical policy of expansion, *la marche interrompue vers les limites de l'ancienne Gaule* (the uninterrupted advance toward the boundaries of ancient Gaul) invisibly guides his every step, with the sole exception that he eschewed such excessively bold methods of force as might have aroused all of Europe against him and cost him his throne, and preferred the modern diplomatic technique of the speculator who would win without risk and conceal questionable practices behind an impressive show window. We have seen how deeply susceptible the Emperor was to all those emotions which have controlled French instincts during the last few generations. In taking the lead, though with cunning reserve, Napoleon stirred up anew the desires which the leader was expected to satisfy. His seed fell upon an all too fertile soil, which was bound in time to produce a harvest of war.

The achievements of the Emperor even in the first act of the drama were important enough. They involved the dissolution of the German Confederation, the very essence of the treaties of 1815, which had hitherto insured the inviolability of German soil. They involved the war for which the Emperor had worked untiringly since 1863—a European situation more favorable to France than any since 1740, in other words, a chaotic condition which cried for a new order. In the second act the Emperor, like almost all Frenchmen, counted upon a victory of Austria; supposedly she was the stronger of the two, and it was Austria whom he had bound in advance by treaty. But as for Prussia, presumably the weaker, which at the very outbreak of the war had been compelled to leave the Rhineland unprotected, it was expected that an emergency would soon arise to compel it to grasp the Emperor's rescuing hand

and fulfill his demands. But even if Austria and Prussia should gradually exhaust one another on the battlefields of Bohemia, and even if the struggle should prove indecisive—which seemed after all the most likely outcome—Napoleon with his fresh forces would be master of the situation, dictating peace to the great and huddling the others together under the wings of the French eagle. Only one possibility was never seriously considered because it seemed too remote, namely that Prussia would emerge as the victor. In that event to be sure the emperor was entirely unprepared from a military point of view and had no treaty to rely upon.

IV

It was of the greatest importance in world history that this event came to pass. After the battle of Königgrätz the war was so definitely decided that, other things being equal, there could be no question as to its final outcome. For the French hopes this meant that the treaty with Austria was now only a scrap of paper and that the dreams of a Rhenish confederation were dissipated before they had even assumed definite shape. That was the thunderclap of Sadowa. It was not primarily a question of the European balance, nor of a new anxiety about a menacing neighbor, nor yet alone of the hurt pride of a nation and an army which for a decade had been looked upon as the leaders in Europe. The first smarting and depressing effect was rather that the Emperor's farsighted game of conquest, in which the whole nation had participated with secret expectations, had been lost; that the great opportunity for the French Rhine policy had come and passed; that it would now be necessary to deal on a footing of equality with a victor who had even before the war refused to enter a bargain; that finally the German national movement, which had been regarded merely as an apple of discord and a pawn in the game, had now became an irresistible force for unity on the very threshold of France, a menace to all the political traditions of France. "We have won Venice for others and lost the Rhine for ourselves," Napoleon confessed to a friend on the evening of July 4. Or was it still possible to resume this game?

Already on the day before Königgrätz Austria had turned to the Emperor and offered to surrender Venetia to France if the Emperor would act as mediator in Germany and Italy on the basis of the agreement of June 12. The object of Austria was to arrange an armistice, to transfer to Bohemia the southern army, released by the withdrawal of Italy from the conflict, and to resume the struggle under these altered conditions, with the possible assistance of France. At the very moment when the Prussian guard was ascending the heights of Chlum and deciding the battle, Napoleon had accepted the position of mediator in principle, but as he was about to exercise it, he had to do so in the light of the decision of Königgrätz. In intervening at that time he must have realized that the distinction of being able to give the combatants the command to cease fighting was a very empty one, unless he could combine it at the same time with a program of French territorial aggrandizement in harmony with the French aims.

Hence at the ministerial council, meeting with the Emperor in the chair on July 5, the day of patriotic tribulations, it was decided to summon the Chambers and have them vote the war credits, and to station 80,000 men on the border for purposes of observation. This first step, which provided for the use of force, would have entailed other steps, especially if Prussia refused mediation. Its purpose would have been to use intervention for forcing great compensations on the Rhine despite Königgrätz.[9] The Emperor decided upon a note which was to announce in the *Moniteur* the convocation of the Chambers, but being at heart undecided, he postponed the signing of the mobilization decree till the next morning. Then, on the evening of July 5, the ministers Rouher and La Valette succeeded in getting him to revoke both steps and to proceed upon a more moderate conciliatory course in keeping with the idea of mediation, instead of at once embarking upon an offensive Rhine policy.

What was the motive for this retraction? Napoleon shied at the first step toward a war which would compromise the ideology of his policy of nationalities and might even lead to a German national war of incalculable dimensions. An arbitrator with so warlike a mien would have had to bear the odium of an offensive war from the very start and at the same time would have courted the considerable danger of war with a European coalition and incurred the enmity of all elements in favor of national revolution. But for a war of this kind, opposed to his previous attitude and to his whole nature, Napoleon was not prepared at this time from a military point of view. That was the deciding factor and explains the surprise of Sadowa. If therefore he decided to assume mediation without a military threat, he hoped, inveterate gambler that he was, that he could avoid a national war and the danger of a coalition and yet exploit the still favorable situation and secure from the good-natured, yielding Prussians a smaller measure of compensations without any great risk.

The inherent difficulties of this course were not inconsiderable. To play the rôle of a mediator and yet to think first of all of his own plans of conquest; to offer Austria all possible aid and support and to grant to Prussia sufficient claims to justify corresponding demands for compensation on the part of France; to assume the rôle of mediator with respect to Prussia and Italy without being able to judge them by the same standards; to sacrifice on the one hand as many middle states (in North Germany) as possible to Prussian annexation and on the other hand to recommend himself to a second group of these states as a savior in time of need—all this in face of the irresistible advance of the Prussians and of the determined, supple parrying of Bismarck. Besides Napoleon was exposed to criticism at home and to hostile reactions abroad. From this maze of problems he was unable to extricate himself so long as he was unwilling to return to the dangerous war policy which he had just avoided. Soon he realized that he was caught in his own well-spun net, and on July 7 the greatly disappointed Austrian ambassador reported that he had never found the Emperor in such a complete state of collapse.

The crisis reached its height when the Prussian conditions of peace were submitted. They included annexations which the Emperor was willing to grant, yes even desired for well known reasons, but they also involved Bismarck's plan for the reform of the Confederation, which had never been taken seriously. The outlines of a German future loomed threateningly on the horizon like a spectre. Were these conditions to be accepted without compensations for France? The Empress herself admitted her tribulations to the Prussian minister. She said: "I shall go to bed as a Frenchwoman and arise as a Prussian." And she took down an atlas to seek a remedy on the map. It was again the old idea of creating between France and Germany a neutral and powerless buffer state. Drouyn de Lhuys also admitted to the Prussian minister that he would strongly advise offering to the Emperor the formation of an independent state consisting of only a small part of the Rhineland and Rhenish Bavaria but belonging to the German Confederation. But Napoleon did not dare to make even these more modest desires a preliminary condition for his sanction of the Prussian peace terms. For if they were rejected he would again be confronted by the question whether their acceptance could be secured by force. After having once refrained from interfering by force, his most ardent desire was to end the war as soon as possible and to carry out, with at least a pretext of solemnity, the rôle of arbitrator, which would have become a source of ridicule if the Prussians had advanced to Vienna. He decided also to leave the question of compensation untouched for the present and by professing a willingness to make concessions, to keep open the possibility of later negotiations in the calmer atmosphere which was sure to follow the preliminaries of peace. And so, goaded by unrest and cheered by secret hopes, he urgently advised the terribly disillusioned Austrians to accept the conditions which meant their withdrawal from the German Confederation and insured the leadership of Prussia in North Germany.

How deeply the French leaders were grieved by this necessary decision appears from the notes which the Empress Eugenie, who still continued to act as the protagonist of action, wrote in reply to the ardent appeals of Prince Metternich. They are full of tears, despair, hope and comfort and run the whole gamut of those emotions which we would expect an unhappy woman to reveal to her deserted lover. "What shall I do?" she wrote on July 11, after the die had been cast. "I have done everything in my power, and in reply they talk of the huge responsibility resting on him who must make the decision. They are not prepared and plead unwillingness to undertake adventures, since they lack the means to support an overt act. My voice is no longer listened to. I am almost alone in my views. They exaggerate the dangers of today in order the better to conceal from their own eyes the dangers of tomorrow. Who knows? Perhaps the game is only delayed. Only this much I can say: that I am sad, but I am powerless. I do not even know what is going on, and all I can reply to you is that the Emperor is doing all he can to secure the best possible peace for you. I am disconsolate and unable to write any more. Ah, if only you could still give them a sound thrashing!"

Only one expedient still remained for the Emperor if in addition to realizing his own hopes he would now check the victorious course of the Prussians and avert the menace of German unity. This consisted in barring the South Germans from the Prussian sphere of power in organizing them in a special group which might eventually become a French sphere of influence. But was it possible to keep North and South Germany apart and to establish two parliaments, as Napoleon dreamed? On the very next day the Emperor, concerned only about the conclusion of peace and his momentary success in the face of public opinion, impressed upon the Prussian minister the view that the *point capital* was that in the new confederation South Germany should if possible be separated from the North, even if this were only an apparent separation. He could not prevent the stipulation of the preliminary treaty which left the relation of North and South Germany to a voluntary mutual agreement. In haste he began to transfer his favor to the southern states which sent intercessors to Paris and yet could not be welcomed with an entirely clear conscience, since some of these very states were specified in the list of compensations which France reserved the right to claim.

In the preliminary peace of Nikolsburg (July 26, 1866), which forlorn Austria accepted at Napoleon's advice, his own defeat was decided. It was not alone a case of one shrewd schemer's being outwitted by a still shrewder schemer—Bismarck—whose success made him appear so. For only a superficial school of historians who merely nibble the edges and never penetrate a subject will see in this contest a duel of two evenly matched methods of diplomacy. Behind these methods there are concealed two different systems of ethics, the incomparability of which we can fully realize today. The policy of Bismarck, in spite of its unmistakable Prussian hue, was, after all, closely bound up with the yearning of a nation to reconstruct itself inwardly and outwardly and to abandon and overcome everything which did not fit into his plan. It was a policy which carried out a historical necessity, but in doing so it had to make use of those methods which were demanded by the general conditions in Europe at that time, and especially by the neighborhood of France. The arts of

Napoleon, on the other hand, steeped in fine slogans, served the sole purpose of interfering in the life-process of another nation. Certainly every innate national egoism, as soon as it enters into relations with other states, will tend to see in the latter only means towards its own ends. But a two-faced scheme such as this, which would make the fate of a great nation the victim of the dynastic ambition of an adventurer, will always offend against the unwritten code of morality which governs the life of states and peoples.

It was the personality and the inmost nature of Napoleon which suffered defeat. To his dismay he realized this. In the days before Nikolsburg he confessed to Count Goltz that he was grateful to King William for having, by moderate means, spared him the humiliation of openly contradicting the policy he had adopted on July 4 and for having at the same time saved him from a policy which could only have ended disastrously for him and his family by conjuring up the spectres of coalition and revolution at the same time. But his spirit now appeared broken. Without mincing words Empress Eugenie revealed to the Austrian ambassador her misgivings over his physical and moral condition. On July 23 she was on the point of advising him to abdicate and to entrust the regency to her, feeling that it would be best if he disappeared for a while.

That was the man who only a few weeks before had gloated vaingloriously over his power to toy with the fate of nations and who was now forced hesitatingly to draw the consequences of his own actions, namely to cajole victorious Prussia into giving him at least a part of what he had failed to get by deceit before the war and had not dared to extract by the sword during the war.

V

THE supposedly favorable moment for action in the matter of compensations, carefully awaited for weeks, came on the day of the preliminary peace. On July 26 in Nikolsburg, Benedetti, still informally, announced the frontiers of 1814 (Saarbrücken, Landau) and the Grand Duchy of Luxemburg as French desiderata. And since an equivalent for Luxemburg would have to be provided for the King of the Netherlands, East Frisia appeared for the first time on the list of German cessions. On the next day Napoleon too mentioned the same subject to the Prussian ambassador, reassuring him by saying that in proposing the frontiers of 1814 and Luxemburg he was interested merely in securing a strategically defensive line.

This gentle prelude was soon followed by more

animated music. Benedetti, apparently as the result of a misunderstanding, had reported his first interview with Bismarck so inaccurately and optimistically to Drouyn de Lhuys that the latter, who had been consumed by impatience during the last few weeks, thought the time ripe for following up this preliminary promising reconnaissance with formal official negotiations,—in the shape of an exceptionally awkward thrust. While the sick Emperor was at Vichy, Drouyn wrung from the heart-broken ruler, apparently by a surprise attack, a list of compensations which, as Bismarck accurately said, would have been possible only if Prussia "had lost the war." Drouyn went so far in his eagerness as to present these claims in Berlin in the form of a draft of a finished treaty. The demands embraced the borders of 1814, Luxemburg, the Bavarian Palatinate and Rhenish Hessia including Mainz.[10] It will be seen that the storm had now moved from the Prussian Rhineland to the territory of the middle states, which according to the treaty of June 12 were to have been so magnanimously enlarged. And how far the present plans went beyond that first feeler! Instead of a modest frontier rectification, great stretches of German territory were now involved, and instead of restricting herself to an alleged line of defence, France reached out for Mainz and for the "keys to Germany" which Thiers had regarded with yearning eyes in 1848. From the military point of view too this was clearly an offensive position. Even those who sought historical parallels had to admit that the demands were entirely incommensurate with the price which Cavour had been obliged to pay for active military support of 1859. And in comparison with the conditions under which Napoleon had offered a war alliance on May 30, the present demands were greater, for although the whole Moselle line was not demanded, yet Mainz was now included in the claim. And all that without any compensation, and after a war in which France, far from having cooperated with Prussia or having earned a reward, had secretly been allied with the other side, and indeed had barely avoided armed intervention against Prussia.

The nature of the claims was in even more direct contradiction to the attitude which Napoleon had hitherto observed in his official and confidential dealings with the Prussian government. It did not harmonize with his theories of nationality nor with his realistic instinct, which appreciated the European dangers of an ambitious offensive policy along the Rhine and with which Bismarck always figured in all his calculations. What was it then that made him believe that in the decisive hour of German victory he could resume Louis XIV's policy of conquest along the upper Rhine and in the midst of peace win the middle Rhine, which revealed most clearly the scars of the ancient struggle between Germany and France? When Voltaire passed through these sections in 1753 he felt a sense of shame for having to pose as an Italian and said: "How could our nation ever be popular here! These ruins are bound to serve as a constant reminder to the people that they have reason to hate everything which is French." But now designing prefects in nearby French provinces again cherished the insane illusion that in those sections over which a wave of radical German nationalism had passed before 1848 a plebiscite would result in a four-fifths majority for France. In the years 1923–1924 the lust of possession conjured up the same illusions.

But what was the psychological explanation of the fact that the Emperor and his minister had yielded so completely to the spirit of July 5? While previously Napoleon, the master of the situation, had toyed with the fate of nations to glorify his own throne, he was now doomed to continue the game for the sake of self-preservation—a slave to the evil spirits he had summoned. Drouyn de Lhuys frankly confessed to the Prussian ambassador that if "genuine" compensations were not secured, both throne and dynasty would be endangered.[11] Thus to the motive of "security," not even mentioned before the war, there was added a motive of fear for the safety of the dynasty, which was hardly worthy of the dispassionate and responsible policy of a great power, the acquisition of German territory being regarded as the only cure for all ills.

From this point of view it is possible to understand the sereneness of Bismarck when Benedetti presented the draft to him in Berlin on August 5, without threatening war but with a hint that a refusal would incur the lasting disfavor of the French government. Bismarck immediately characterized the demand as inacceptable and out of the question, certain in his conviction that he was championing the cause of a nation which, having just emerged from civil war, was eager to present a united front to the outside world and to defend its right of self-determination and the inviolability of its soil against the dynastic ambitions of all its neighbors. Even had he been willing personally to yield a small fraction of the exaggerated maximum demands, Prussian honor and the self-consciousness of the nation would both have prevented his doing so. He knew that King William, returned from a victorious war, would adhere all the more faithfully to his dictum of 1860 that he would never consent to the surrender of a single German hamlet. Hence Bismarck replied forthwith that any consideration of the French demand would cause extreme excitement throughout Germany and would be fatal to Prussia's position in Germany. He informed his ambassador in Paris that if Napoleon motivated the demand on the basis of consideration for his country and public opinion, Prussia would use the same arguments in reply. Like a flash there passed through Bismarck's mind the thought of calling upon the nation in case of great emergency and, as he later confessed to Carl Schurz, to unleash a national war in the spirit of the Frankfurt constitution of 1849 the very thought of which would make Napoleon shudder. But actually he took advantage of the opportunity to persuade the South German states threatened by France to conclude peace speedily and to enter offensive and defensive alliances with Prussia. To achieve this, considerable concessions were necessary. Confronted by the need of studying the future of the German relations to France, the Prussian statesman became aware of the truly national character of his action and assumed a thoroughly German point of view more quickly perhaps than he had originally planned. If his opponents later reproached him with having violated the letter and spirit of the Nikolsburg preliminaries while the peace negotiations were still under way, they forgot that by their own demands they had forced him to take this measure of defence. However, Napoleon, who had but recently posed as the friend of the German middle states, gambled away his German policy at this juncture, and to the Germans he seemed a diabolical force unwittingly working good while plotting evil.

The crisis lasted only a few days, for Napoleon who, as it was, had been driven further than he really wished by his wife and minister soon retreated before the unconditional resistance of Berlin. But even before he could retreat, Drouyn de Lhuys himself, the real author of the plan, had hit upon another expedient which never led to more than a minor episode but is characteristic of the political thought of these circles. A memorial of the minister set forth with the irrefutable formal logic which the Gallic mind is fond of employing to prove that its illusions are the dictates of reason, that France does not cherish the ambition of subjecting people of different nationality to her own rule and that it is solely the motive of security and national defence which demands a revision of the boundaries. The formation of a neutral state embracing the entire left bank of the Rhine (Prussian, Bavarian and Hessian territory),[12] guaranteed by the neighboring powers and "politically separated from the new Germany which Prussia wished to create, but spiritually still a part of it" would satisfy this demand, he said. And if the new throne were offered to the hereditary prince Leopold of Hohenzollern-Sigmaringen, he believed this would be dynastically a satisfactory solution for King William too and would prove honorable for all concerned. Otherwise, he added, the French instinct of self-preservation would react irresistibly against the Prussian power, which had become a constant menace, and the wisdom of the governments would be powerless to curb the passions which stirred the two nations against one another. On the other hand the creation of a neutral buffer state would give France, and Germany too, a feeling of immunity from attack.

Whether this proposal, which revived the old favorite thought of Napoleon, had the approval of the Emperor at this time is not certain. At any rate it reached Berlin only through unofficial channels and was summarily rejected in Bismarck's antechamber. But the episode characterizes the unchanged attitude of French diplomacy toward the development of Germany and the incorrigibility of a policy which, even when receding from the idea of the territorial acquisition of the *petit Rhin*, reverts to the idea of the neutralization of the *grand Rhin*, and, appearing suddenly in the guise of Hohenzollern dynastic interests, alights with impressive irony upon the hereditary prince Leopold as the future guarantor of international conciliation. The arguments have changed in the course of the last few centuries, but the objectives have remained the same. So too the old motive of aggrandizement, which had previously used the formula of compensations, now finds a different pretext in the appealing and easily intelligible argument of concern for national security.

But meanwhile the Emperor, under the influence of the minister Rouher, had decided to get rid of Drouyn de Lhuys entirely and to abandon his policy of German compensations in favor of a completely different course. The change came so suddenly that the Empress Eugenie, still the ally of the minister, sought to justify this new retreat in detail to Prince Metternich. "The occasion is a poor one for war," she wrote to him on August 13. "You must first heal your wounds and we must be ready. Either we must undertake nothing or be sure of all possible chances for success. Is that equivalent to robbing you of your confidence? Far from it. On the contrary, the time will come and then—who knows? But meanwhile I think it lies in your interest as well as in ours to allow no distrust to arise in Prussia and to hasten no circumstances which might prove fatal for us all. Once France takes up the idea of the Rhine, believe me, she will follow out this idea as persistently as you would follow out another . . ." [13] In thus receding for the sake of getting a better start the next time, the throne once more attached itself to the "idea" which had dominated all these years, though in this case it was merely a question of giving prostrate Austria a new hope for the future.

But the principal feature of the new idea which replaced the old program was that it sought compensations not so much on German soil as in Belgium. A memorial prepared for the Emperor by Rouher on August 15 began with the significant words: "If France takes a bold stand on the basis of nationalities, it is now important to establish the principle that no Belgian nationality exists and to formulate this decisive point together with Prussia." [14] [15] It stressed the fact that the Prussians must be convinced that the Emperor was not seeking his necessary territorial acquisitions on the Rhine and that a treaty on this basis would have the twofold advantage of compromising Prussia and giving it a pledge for the honest intentions of the Emperor. Napoleon adopted this proposal without hesitation. It appeared to be the only bridge to span the chasm of defeat. On the very next day Benedetti received his instructions. He was to proceed amicably and without any threat, and he was to take the following steps:

first to demand the boundaries of 1814 and Luxemburg and—in a secret treaty—Belgium; then in case of opposition to abandon Saarbrücken, Saarlouis and even the "drab old town of Landau," the loss of which would only stir up the German people anyhow, and to content himself with the program of an open treaty on Luxemburg and a secret one on Belgium (if absolutely necessary Antwerp was to be made a free port). On August 19 Benedetti submitted to the German premier the draft of a treaty written in his own hand and based on these instructions.[16] It combined the cession of Luxemburg, the agreement on Belgium and the French sanction of a national union between North and South Germany. With impatient urging from one day to the next—as if a mere diplomatic trifle and not a momentous decision were involved—he sought in a trice to get the consent of Bismarck and his king.

Thus France had signified her willingness to accept German unification as an accomplished fact and, renouncing the compensations on the Rhine (with the exception of Luxemburg), to abandon not only the German states which she had volunteered to protect, but also the idea of a Rhenish confederation. But she consented to this only on condition that she might with impunity disturb the peace of Europe at another point and on the further condition that

Prussia should formally and from the very beginning make herself an accomplice and advocate of this disturbance. It is the old spirit necessarily seeking some different outlet which seems more accessible. By aiming at the annexation of Belgium instead of the Rhineland, the new scheme merely emphasized another phase of the old program whose reaction upon the security of the German left bank would be practically certain. The new objective was the northern section of the bulwark erected in 1815 by the powers, but maintained only in the shape of Belgian neutrality since 1830. The French later objected that the diabolical Bismarck had been the real proponent of the Belgian motive, having brought it up in order to tempt the French, and that the incautious Benedetti had written the notorious treaty draft more or less at Bismarck's dictation. In reality the political imagination of France had ever since the 'thirties been toying with the idea of annexing neutralized Belgium, thus breaking down the Belgian bulwark. We have already noted that the plan was one of Napoleon's dreams for the future. Hence if Bismarck, in the precarious situation of the summer of 1866 and in the face of the French designs upon German territory, referred France to French linguistic territory for the satisfaction of her desires, he merely did his duty from the point of view of his own state.

Under the pressure of circumstances he exploited the existing Belgian aspirations of France as a lightning rod to protect his own house from disaster. But when, as a result of the French initiative, the situation suddenly became serious, he immediately realized the import of the proposal and his responsibility to Europe as well as to Germany.

Even the instruction with which the ambassador Count Goltz returned to Paris on September 7, pointed out definite limits in spite of all its cordiality. In friendly words Prussia declared herself ready to foster international understanding and—provided Napoleon would assume a similar attitude toward Prussia's program for a German national state—to observe a friendly neutrality toward France in her effort to extend her power by acquiring French territory. But the initiative and all measures looking toward the "maturition" of this question were left to Napoleon. If obstacles and dangers should arise later, Prussia would gladly be prepared to enter discussions. By postponing a contractual agreement for the time being, Prussia really rejected the essence of the French overtures. It accepted no responsibility and no share of the risk. It is not surprising then that Paris was disappointed. Especially Rouher, the chief advocate of the new course, spoke not only of the requirements of security and of the internal situation, but added with grave concern that in case of refusal the Emperor's only recourse would be to revert to the policy of Drouyn de Lhuys. He predicted that otherwise the national passions and hatreds would lead to a war of incalculable consequences, yes even to a whole series of wars. He conjured up the spectre of a world war if France failed to obtain the treaty and with it Belgium and Luxemburg. It is no wonder that King William, in his straightforward, conscientious manner wrote under the ambassador's report the following words: "It is the same old tendency: Prussia is to save Napoleon, as it were, and conclude a secret treaty in order to conspire against an innocent and friendly nation . . . If Germany were ever to learn that I had entered a French alliance for the destruction of Belgium, in order thereby to win the upper hand in Germany, the German sympathies would disappear considerably." [17] Here was an insurmountable barrier which would have made it impossible for Bismarck partially to sanction Napoleon's plan even had he so desired.

But Paris insisted all the more impatiently upon an immediate decision on the proposed treaty because it was planned to issue a proclamation for the purpose of quieting the public mind. This proclamation was to give the main outline of the new French foreign policy, in particular the attitude toward the situation in Germany, and to illuminate this policy by giving a few significant hints as to the future. Such was the circular instruction of La Valette of September 16. Since the diplomatic tactics of Bismarck strove to avoid an outright rupture, he found himself hard pressed by the insistence of the French on the one side and the determined attitude of the King on the other. He had to resort to dilatory methods, until toward the middle of September, an indisposition which developed into a more serious illness early in October—perhaps a result of the superhuman strain of the past year—came very providentially. At any rate the negotiations were interrupted for several months.

These negotiations were resumed when Bismarck returned from Rügen to Berlin early in December and set to work upon the constitution of the North German Confederation. The new foreign minister Marquis Moustier in Paris and Benedetti in Berlin now began to press more strenuously for a decision. Early in January, 1867, the Emperor and Rouher seriously took part in their efforts. In view of Bismarck's renewed evasiveness Moustier now resorted to more impressive oral arguments. He said that an alliance was to be preferred to the chances of a war which if unfavorable for Prussia would mean the loss of the left bank of the Rhine, and that as long as possible he would avoid an *alliance bâtarde* with Austria and South Germany. He added that the Prussian victories had aroused the French army to a desire to measure its strength against the Prussian army. *Nous sommes des coqs* he openly admitted. It was natural that Bismarck, who in the days of the foundation of the new German state had at the same time to reach a decision on the course of its foreign policy, became more and more suspicious of this ally. "Let them not forget in Paris," an order of December 20 to Goltz read, "that there can be an alliance in our sense of the word only between equals and between states which respect and have consideration for one another, that we refuse to purchase the alliance, and that if they set a price upon it which we can not pay now, they will be forcing us into other channels which we are not only able to take, but into which we are being invited." Thus Bismarck worked harder than ever to give the plan a defensive instead of an offensive character.

On the other hand, January, 1867, seems to mark a turning point in the French policy. Napoleon was secretly approaching Austria again, and early in February he made the significant statement that he desired Austria to recover her position in Germany. But in the negotiations with Prussia diminishing emphasis was placed upon the alliance and Belgium (although the formal negotiations were still continued), and greater stress laid upon the "Luxemburg question," which was claimed to be disturbing public opinion. The surrender of the former confederate fortress in which the Prussian garrison was still stationed gradually became paramount, but not so much as a link in a new system of alliances, as an isolated conpensation—as a last residuum of the claims of 1866. Although Bismarck had acknowledged no far-reaching obligations in the past, he saw no particular gain in holding Luxemburg and regarded Prussia's right to maintain a garrison there open to question. But he considered it advisable to issue a warning against excessive haste in such a delicate matter, because the fortress could be surrendered only on condition that this would not compromise Prussia's position in Germany and that the insignificant move would not cost the king the sympathies of Germany. For this reason he refused to take the initiative and suggested that demonstrations in Luxemburg demanding the dismantling of the fort and an initial step on the part of The Hague must be the first necessary stage. Although the French had up to now emphasized the purely defensive aspect, they refused steadfastly to discuss dismantling. They wanted the fortress itself. Bismarck formulated the question as follows: Only if we are convinced that

France will continue the policy of September 16, i. e. absolute sanction of the German national movement, can we agree to renounce such a fortress as Luxemburg. Moustier issued a formal declaration that Napoleon had no ambitions along the Rhine, yet he hinted that France would be completely satisfied only by the surrender of Luxemburg, which was already described as *terre française*, and that this would assure peace for some years. Hence it was natural that the other side began to ask whether the surrender of Luxemburg would not after all be but a drop in the bucket.

No matter from what point of view the matter might be considered, it was unquestionably intertwined with the general question of the future relations of Germany and France. And these relations were no longer in Napoleon's hands alone; they depended too on public opinion, which was criticising the failures of his policy more and more. Returning from a journey in Southern France early in March, 1867, Prince Metternich expressed the opinion "that the whole country is animated by a single feeling, and that is hatred for Prussia. Everywhere people are conscious of the mistakes which have been made and of the great opportunity which would never return. They yearn for a *revanche éclatante*.[18] This feeling became more intense when after March

8 the conclusion of offensive and defensive alliances between Prussia and the southern states was divulged and caused consternation instead of a more sober attitude, for which Bismarck had hoped. The French saw in the alliances, which were in reality the outgrowth of their own cupidity, a symbol of the perfidious German striving for unification. They began to grasp the problematic character of the Main line, which—as Bismarck said at this time—"is not a real wall but an ideal boundary and in a sense a fence through which the national current, whose irresistible trend had to be acknowledged in the *liens nationaux*, makes its way." Could this current be halted? When in the *Corps législatif* impatient legislators asked about the status of the Luxemburg question, Bismarck said that a fortress like Luxemburg could not be surrendered for the sake of making a good momentary impression upon a legislature, that the price was too high for this purpose but not sufficient to modify the warlike spirit among the people and in the army.

Under these circumstances the crisis came. The imperial government had since the end of February created the impression that it would act upon Bismarck's advice, but as a matter of fact it ignored his elastic hints and reservations by hasty and disloyal conduct. It was thought necessary to confront the

Prussian government with an accomplished fact, and while the Prussian garrison was still in Luxemburg the government concluded a treaty of cession with the King of the Netherlands. When the latter notified King William on March 26, the crisis was on. The ill-considered game of the French had created a situation which was in direct contradiction to Bismarck's careful hints. During these weeks in which the first North German Reichstag had met to consider the constitution of the Confederation, a strong wave of German national feeling might have been recognized as inevitable in case the surrender of a fortress belonging to the Confederation seriously threatened. And so Bismarck decided to submit the question at the same time to Europe and to the German nation. His answer, that he would appeal to the contracting parties of 1839, the German governments and the North German Confederation, was necessarily regarded in Paris as equivalent to a refusal.

Now the waves of passion and disappointment rose high. At first it was declared that a retreat was no longer possible, even after the Reichstag debates of April 2 had lifted the veil from the threatening danger. Even the official circles said that Bismarck had set a trap and that they would not shun a war for the sake of getting control of Luxemburg. But especially after the King of the Netherlands had withdrawn from the affair, the diplomatic situation of France became very unfavorable. Not only Gorchakov considered it unworthy of a great power to seek in Luxemburg a pretext for war, but even Beust and Metternich condemned the action of French diplomacy. Since the French were not prepared for war anyway, Napoleon decided to accept a compromise and for the present to bury the last remnant of his claim for compensation. After several tense weeks both sides accepted the mediation of the powers. To Moltke, who clamored for a decision, Bismarck replied: "One should not wage war when it can be honorably avoided; bright prospects for success do not constitute a just motive for beginning a war." And so in the third week of April the crisis blew over. On May 11 the conference of the powers in London found the solution which provided that Luxemburg be separated from the Confederation and the Prussian garrison removed, but also that the fortress be dismantled and that the territory, as a neutralized state, should retain its dynastic affiliation with the Netherlands. That was the end of this French claim for compensation.

In renouncing Luxemburg, French diplomacy turned back just as suddenly and unostentatiously as before to its old Rhine policy. At the very time that he accepted the proposals for mediation Napoleon hinted to the Austrian ambassador that his readiness to agree to a compromise in principle did not exclude the possibility of an offensive war immediately or later. From the disclosures which the Emperor and Empress made to Prince Metternich on April 16, the latter inferred that the Duke of Gramont, who had been called to Paris, would return to Vienna with an array of indiscreet and characteristic questions. Again Eugenie, as usual the seductive advance guard, took down her famous map, which had so often been consulted and laid aside (the superstitious Metternich remarked that fortunately the old copy had been stolen), and asked the ambassador, who refused to build another castle in the air with her, to reply at least to the following question: What would Austria gain by an alliance with France in case of war? In her projects she outdid herself in trying to satisfy the future partner.

On April 23 Gramont in two long conversations reported to Baron Beust the upshot of the new French speculations. Instructed at first to ascertain the lay of the land, he then spoke freely in accordance with his orders. He offered nothing less than an offensive and defensive alliance with far-reaching war aims. Austria and France were to bind themselves not to lay down their arms until they had attained certain objectives. For Napoleon they included the left bank of the Rhine, "which he proposed to acquire," especially the Bavarian Palatinate, [Rhenish Hessia] and that part of the Rhineland situated left of the Rhine. On the other hand Austria was to receive Silesia and could make any arrangements in South Germany she pleased, forming a confederation under its own leadership or making suitable annexations—but with the understanding that France was interested in the fate of the Grand Duchy of Baden.[19] On the ridge of the Black Forest, it appears, the French and Austrian spheres of influence were to meet, according to this visionary scheme.

The French proposal never got very far because Beust immediately turned down this "somewhat adventuresome plan" and maintained his position even after Gramont had indicated that in case of refusal France would negotiate with Russia or even with Prussia—at Austria's expense, of course. But Beust pointed to the internal difficulties of the Monarchy, especially to the aversion of the German Austrians against participating in a war which had "the admitted purpose" of subjecting a part of Germany to foreign rule. He refused to consider an alliance upon so unfavorable a basis and with such unconcealed offensive aims.

Regardless of its rejection the French offer is a document of permanent historical value. Embittered over the setback in Luxemburg and eager to find some other ally, Paris had dropped all diplomatic sham. Even the Napoleonic theory of nationalities was jettisoned. What had been designated cautiously and by degrees in the negotiations before the war and later in the compensation claim, was now openly summarized—no longer in the uncomfortable disguise of a buffer state but in its true light of conquest and aggrandizement. The Rhine frontier no longer sufficed; where it was already a reality it was ruthlessly crossed. So rapidly had the comforting prediction of Empress Eugenie of August 13, 1866, come true: "When once France takes up the idea of the Rhine frontier . . ." The traditional French policy of conquest was once more the order of the day. These were the days of the adoption of the constitution of the North German Confederation, the basis of the constitution of the German Empire which was to follow. But while the nation, deeply stirred, marched on to unity, its body and soul were still being used as pawns in the game of dynastic ambition and foreign greed.

During these days Bismarck correctly said: "The menace to peace lies not in Luxemburg's value for France or for the Emperor, but rather in the readiness with which the latter submits to the greedy instincts of the French nation and in his desire to avert trouble at home by successes abroad." Indeed the closest military confidant of the Emperor, General Fleury, confessed at the beginning of the Luxemburg crisis: "If only the Prussians do not yield. For us war is the only possible way out of this general chaos. It will prevent the complete disruption of France and the overthrow of the dynasty by hostile parties." Although Eugenie said to Prince Metternich on April 11 that neither she nor the Emperor were wedded to the throne, except for the purpose of defeating the Prussians in battle and then transferring the reins of the government to some successor, without compromising French honor and fame, yet in reality they wished to retain the throne for themselves and their son. Precisely this concern impelled the Emperor to abandon completely his former sober convictions, which had always served to dampen his extreme ardor. The same anxiety was at the bottom of his new policy and was destined to drive him onward to July, 1870, despite his secret misgivings. The truth was that the insecurity of the Second Empire, born of a *coup d'état* and of crime, had developed into a menace to the peace of Europe.

Even if it were granted that the French offer of an alliance was only a grand gesture to conceal from Austria the retreat which had begun, and that at this moment Napoleon counted neither upon a rupture nor upon an acceptance on Austria's part, this would hardly alter the symptomatic import of his step. The Parisian policy had revealed itself to the Austrians quite deliberately and had shown at least for the future the extensive objective with which an eventual ally of France would have to reckon. With respect to the inchoate German state France had once more proved that she favored a policy of offensive intervention.

One of Bismarck's despatches, dated April 18, voiced a different sentiment. "Germany has no desire to conquer, it has not enlarged itself and demands nothing from France; it has only acquired a new and better organization by internal struggles and has even suffered a diminution of its strength through the exclusion of Austria! But it is prepared to guard against any unwarranted interference." France had made precisely such interference a part of her program. At the very time that France turned to Austria, punitive pressure was brought to bear upon the largest German middle state because it seemed inclined, under Prince Hohenlohe's leadership, to get into closer contact with the North German Confederation. The Bavarian government, which during the crisis had used the Tauffkirchen mission to open roads both to Vienna and Berlin, was informed by Paris that if it adhered to this attitude, the final peace in case of war would be made on Bavaria's back (*sur le dos de la Bavière*). This sounds very much like the old domineering language used by the First Empire to its vassals. The German middle states always served Parisian diplomacy merely as a means to an end, depending upon the way the wind blew. They were either objects of its hunger for compensation, or precious wards, and were offered now to Prussia and now to Austria. Perhaps, indeed, the French proffer of an alliance to Austria was meant primarily as a counter-blast to the Tauffkirchen mission.

After the war of 1866 as well as before it, French diplomacy traveled in the path of the old traditional Rhine policy, without any broad European vision. Meanwhile a new generation was arising in Germany which expected a unified national state to protect it against foreign enemies. The Germans wanted only self-determination, while the French could not abandon their national tendency to intervene in German affairs and their historical Rhine policy. Such is the clue to the succeeding years.

VI

AFTER the Luxemburg crisis Napoleon's policy had no alternative. Instead of his former toying with various possibilities, he now had only one aim, and in place of the free hand which had once quite arbitrarily tampered with the European states system, there was now only the dire necessity of subverting a part of that system at any cost. This motive determined his whole foreign policy, especially his policy of alliance, during the next few years. Although its pace changed frequently, the policy itself remained constant, for it had but a single impulse.

The intense excitement of the spring of 1867 was followed by a quiet summer. It was the time of the World's Fair in Paris—a gigantic exposition with its true Parisian admixture of art and display, of women and pleasure, of music and parades, in the midst of which high society as well as the *demi monde* lent a colorful touch to the last bright days of the Second Empire, while the visits of European royalty for the last time set off the court of Napoleon in its old splendor. But political activity, which played even into these festivities, was only temporarily relaxed. Prince Gorchakov who accompanied Tsar Alexander did indeed make earnest efforts to vouch for the future moderation of Bismarck's German policy and King William and Bismarck on their part gave the assurance that they would not press the southern states further. But Napoleon confessed to the Russians that during the last crisis he was astounded at the vehemence with which war against

Prussia was demanded on every side, and that if Prussia were even to consider establishing garrisons in the former confederate fortresses of Rastatt and Ulm, this would mean war. And although the Prussians were received, outwardly at least, with respectful curiosity, they continually sensed hidden aspirations everywhere. When Bismarck spoke to Marshal Canrobert on the policy of nationalities, the latter, according to his own words, had the constant thought: "We know of a province on the left bank of the Rhine which at heart though not in language is French," and said nothing. The eternal schemer Persigny showed himself more aggressive in his attitude toward Bismarck, urging him to save the endangered peace of the nations by having Prussia make further annexations in North Germany, especially of Saxony, and placing the King of Saxony on the throne of a neutral Rhenish state. The minister Moustier contented himself with the hint of a suggestion that Luxemburg be excluded from the German Zollverein.

It was in connection with this latter point that the slowly increasing tension was aggravated. Immediately before leaving for Paris Bismarck had concluded negotiations with the southern states for the renewal of the customs union treaties and for the completion of the union by the establishment of a customs parliament. In this way he strengthened the economic unity of Germany which had been disturbed by the war. But hardly had King William and his minister left Paris when the excitement of the Parisian press, checked with difficulty during their stay, broke forth anew with charges that Prussian policy was once more overstepping all the bounds of peace and existing treaties. Moustier himself, who now made no secret of his irritation, charged the customs treaties, like the offensive and defensive alliances of August 1866 with violating the letter and spirit of the Treaty of Prague. In their stead, he frankly said, the Prussians should have restricted themselves to a North German Zollverein which could then have concluded commercial treaties with an eventual South German Zollverein as with other powers. In particular he charged the customs parliament with being a political institution. He asked why the seat of this customs parliament, if such an institution were necessary at all, had not been established elsewhere than in Berlin—to the Bavarian minister he recommended Würzburg, or Bamberg! —and why new indirect elections or, still better, elections by the chambers of commerce, had not been provided for instead of letting the South German delegates enter the North German Reichstag. In the same schoolmaster's tone of voice he berated the

South Germans for having become vassals of Prussia, and the Bavarians for having abandoned their original opposition to the Zollverein, and the Württembergers for not having joined Baden and Hessia in supporting Bavaria.

All in all these complaints and reproaches make a memorable document testifying to the persistent desire of the French to interfere in Germany. While at the Paris Exposition they uttered many words anent the conciliatory power of economic and technical forces, they did not refrain from bold interference with the rudimentary right of their neighbor to shape his own economic destinies. Although the economic unity of Germany (exclusive of Austria) in the Zollverein had been a recognized fact for decades, Paris now pretended that the line of the Main should, in accordance with the Treaty of Prague, be applied to the economic sphere too. If the Germans, unwilling to sacrifice everything they had gained since 1834, insisted upon maintaining their customs unity, Paris dictated that this could be done only in such a way as not to ruffle the French sensibilities. The extreme arrogance underlying these outbursts led to no official steps for the present, but they betrayed the ever renewed though impotent feeling of resentment on account of the defeat of 1866, and the desperate attempt to make of the Treaty of

Prague a legal instrument whereby the development of the German national state could be arrested from without. What presumptuous language the French dared to use when they felt it necessary to bring neighborly pressure to bear, is shown by the conduct of the French minister in Karlsruhe, who gave special emphasis to his warnings by such phrases as "We who created the Grand Duchy of Baden"—as if the days of the Rhenish Confederation could have been recreated in those days, and as if such allusions were not bound to injure the feelings of a nation ripe for unity.

The French policy, symptoms of which were at first recognizable only in such outbursts, but were also expressed in sharper reminders of North Schleswig, was designed to provide a basis for deliberation in conjunction with the expected visit of the Emperor Francis Joseph, and if possible to provide a starting point for common action. But since Francis Joseph's visit was canceled on account of the tragedy of Emperor Maximilian in Mexico, Napoleon postponed his action until his visit of condolence to Salzburg from August 18 to 22. The Salzburg meeting was arranged from the first for the express purpose of resuming the almost tumultuous effort of April, 1867, for rapprochement, and of promoting the matter by a personal interview of the monarchs and their advisers. In fact Beust counted in advance upon an offer of alliance. He said: "I am sure I am right in assuming that in this case the acquisition of German territory by France would be mentioned in the alliance as an express purpose." But in view of the internal situation of Austria, he was as firmly resolved as he had been four months before, to avoid such far-reaching obligations.

Meetings of monarchs and their personal interviews are generally shrouded in a darkness which trustworthy sources do not always illuminate sufficiently. Although the actual results of Salzburg, in keeping with Beust's policy, were modest, the decisive point is not what the French actually attained but what they tried to get from Austria. Beust himself later admitted in confidence to his Darmstadt friend Baron von Dalwigk that at Salzburg Napoleon offered him South Germany in return for the left bank of the Rhine. Indeed a document of this character has been preserved, the authenticity of which is certain though the authorship and its place in the discussions is not clear. On the basis of Beust's memoirs it is reasonable to think of the Duke of Gramont who was present in Salzburg. In this project [20] an active alliance between France and Austria was proposed for the purpose of enforcing the strict observance of the Treaty of Prague on Prussia's part.

Strict observance included no less than the following: cancelation of the offensive and defensive alliances, formation of a southern confederation under the joint auspices of Austria and France, with the parliamentary seat in Vienna, and with the same rights for the Emperor of Austria as Prussia possessed in the North German Confederation; evacuation of the fortress of Mainz by the Prussians and secession of Upper Hessia from the Confederation; finally the establishment of an Austro-South German Zollverein. In case Prussia refused to sanction this program, both Austria and France were to declare war, the objectives of which were to be: for France only the frontiers of 1814 and for Austria Upper Silesia. Moreover the territory annexed by Prussia in 1866 was to decide by plebiscite not only its form of government, but also its membership in the North German Confederation. Lastly Art. 5 of the Treaty of Prague was to be enforced jointly by the two powers. The two powers pretended that they were championing the independence of the southern states in conformity with the Treaty of Prague, but if these states refused to conclude the alliance suggested to them, they were to be forced by an ultimatum or by war and then be punished by loss of territory.

All this represents the second effort of a bellicose power, which would strike the moment it had an ally. The program of this intervention, closely connected with the April offer and the disputes of the summer, breathes the old French spirit which had consistently treated the German nation as a tool in its struggle for power. So far as restricting themselves to the boundaries of 1814 is concerned, the French agreed to this only because Austria refused to sign an agreement in advance sanctioning French annexations. But even so the project was not acceptible to the Austro-Hungarian Monarchy, which needed peace and was far from ready for action. Beust was by no means prepared to act as the accomplice to such a flagrant interference in the German question on the part of a foreign power. He turned down the proffers and achieved an agreement which above all stipulated a joint Far Eastern policy as the basis for closer relations between the two powers. Warlike intervention in Germany was rejected in favor of a more diplomatic method: by following a policy of reserve the national party was to be deprived of every pretext for action, while the middle states were to be strengthened in their resistance; Austria was to establish a new moral influence and Bismarck's policy was to be shrewdly but effectively thwarted. If Napoleon at Salzburg dropped his ambitious plans in favor of this program of peace, he did so under pressure and in the hope that as soon as Austria had recovered from the war of 1866, she could by force of circumstances be maneuvered out of her present state of inactivity.

And so Salzburg too remained a mere episode, like the April proposal, but it was the first step toward a closer understanding of the two powers. The return visit of Francis Joseph to Paris in November served to strengthen it without extending it. Although the fears which the meeting rightfully aroused in South Germany were not realized—the idea of a southern confederation was confronted by insurmountable difficulties—one result at least was clear. For the first time since the summer of 1866 a gentle pressure was brought to bear upon the South German states by Paris and Vienna combined, and the stronger it grew, the more certain was its effect. Both in Munich and Stuttgart an effort was made to steer a more conservative course on account of the gathering clouds. It seemed as if the customs union treaties of 1867 represented the utmost limits of possible achievement. But those particularistic elements in Germany which opposed unification for reasons of self-interest or obstinacy began to take advantage of the favorable wind coming from abroad —a bad habit not uncommon to the Germans.

Napoleon's next task was to conform to Beust's plan, whose effectiveness he realized, but at the same time to make every effort to steer Austrian polity gradually into a more active course in harmony with that of France. Hence the French government evaded the attempt of the Vienna cabinet (early in 1868) to use a threatened crisis in the Near East for the purpose of recreating, as it were, by a triple alliance between Austria, France and Great Britain, the situation of the Crimean War. Not the Near East but only Germany could henceforth be a fitting objective for French diplomacy, and the continued unsettled state of the German situation seemed favorable for exercising the joint influence of the two powers to the full.

With this and only this end in view the new army organization of Marshal Niel was carried through. It was discussed in the chambers during the spring of 1868 and inflamed public opinion with a martial fire. The prominent military men assumed leadership in the movement which aimed at spurring the Emperor on. When Prince Metternich took part in the discussions of the Emperor and his generals at Compiegne in January, 1868, he felt as if he were attending "a secret council of war." Fleury, Ney and Niel assured him openly that "the Emperor was so secretly planning measures against his domestic and foreign enemies behind the backs of his peace ministers, that France and Europe would in a very short time, be surprised at his thorough preparedness for any eventuality." [21] Whoever reads the memoirs of Ducrot and examines the letters of Bazaine and Bourbaki must realize that the whole French military group was animated by a single thought. Especially Ducrot belonged to those who passionately demanded action and a resumption of the Rhine policy by the Emperor. From Strassburg he undertook trips with his staff into Baden and when he came from his secret observations in Mainz to Darmstadt, he was a welcome guest at the Grand Duke's court. In the camp of the opposition the same spirit prevailed, as may be seen from the book of Charles Muller *Nos frontières sur le Rhin* (April, 1868), which, glorifying the Bourbons, described in broad outline the history of the French ambitions along the Rhine since 1815, and ended by appealing to Napoleon to realize the desire of the nation and make France the master of the Rhine from Strassburg to Cologne. The work culminated in a paean in praise of war as the great creative force and the supreme motive power in human progress. In this very fact lay the inevitability of the decisions with which the Emperor was confronted: on the one side the anti-Napoleonic parties, Legitimists, Orleanists, Republicans, who scathingly criticised his failures and called upon the Empire to prove its worth to the nation; on the other hand those who were allied with the cause of the empire by birth or interest, one and all calling ever more loudly for action for their own sake, for the sake of the dynasty, and for the sake of France. Even if Napoleon did not want war —and prior to the conclusion of an effective alliance he could hardly want it—, he had to give freer play to the idea in view of his entourage and his own inclinations. His closest advisers were already beginning to construe his enigmatic silence as a sign of coming war. The English ambassador in a confidential private letter to Queen Victoria, written late in March (it found its way to Berlin too), reported that although the language of the French ministers was very pacific, intimate students of Napoleon's character concluded from various symptoms that he was harboring the thought of suddenly declaring war against Prussia. He had, to be sure, not reached a final decision but was proceeding quietly without revealing his plans to any one, so that when the suitable moment arrived he could take Prussia by surprise and at the same time carry French public opinion by storm.[22]

The high tension which gradually disturbed all Europe was closely connected with the German situation. Toward the end of March, 1868, the elections for the customs parliament had taken place in South

Germany. On April 27 this parliament was to convene in Berlin. A turn in events seemed imminent. Prince Napoleon had returned from a reconnoitering tour in Berlin, which was partly to serve as a warning and was partly intended to seek concessions, and he brought back the conviction that German unity could no longer be arrested. He too spoke to his friends openly of war. Was it not possible that the Prussian government or the customs parliament itself might attempt to enlarge its sphere and tend to become a national parliament? Or was it still possible to encourage, by further support from Paris, the German particularistic elements, who to the joy of the French had asserted themselves successfully in the elections?

At this moment Emperor Napoleon decided to resume the Salzburg policy and to try once more to win Austria over to active participation with France. He began by asking Prince Metternich on April 7, 1868 what Vienna intended to do if the South Germans should voluntarily take Prussia's side or if Prussia should violate the Treaty of Prague and force the South Germans to side with it. As usual the Duc de Gramont expressed himself still more vehemently in Vienna, saying that France would regard the crossing of the Main line as a *casus belli* and that whereas she had formerly not been prepared, she was now ready to strike. What was to be expected of Austria? When Beust temporized and evaded the question and spoke of neutrality, the vehement Frenchman replied: "Then we will drag you along with us." So, at least, with careful calculation he boasted to the Bavarian minister, giving him to understand that then Bavaria too would be called upon to decide between the rôles of friend and foe. From day to day the odor of powder emanating from Paris grew stronger in Europe. Warlike utterances of Niel and other ministers were the subject of common gossip; military measures were openly taken; the arrival of the Danish minister of war in Paris was noted; and general opinion had it that the war would begin in July or August. Officious agents hastened from Paris to Vienna and back, stopping at Darmstadt en route to speak quite candidly of war plans and schedules. It is impossible to lift the veil completely from these shady proceedings, which have left only faint traces in the official documents, but it is certain that the impetuous urging of the French was again confronted by cautious reserve on the part of the Austrians.

All this does not prove that Napoleon wanted war at this time, and indeed it is not likely that he did. But it is certain that he took advantage of the clamor to intimidate the customs parliament and the South

German governments and utilized the acute tension to draw Austria closer to himself. He actually succeeded in getting Beust to write a note to Berlin which issued a stern warning that if the customs parliament overstepped its competency, this would give the Austrian government just cause for concern, in which case Austria would be more than an uninterested spectator. The moderate attitude of the customs parliament and the pacific policy of Bismarck soon dispelled the crisis. Bismarck had enough sense of realities and of responsibility not to hasten matters. With the calmness which comes of confidence in the future and which is a remarkable contrast to the nervous sabre-rattling of the French, he declared to the chief of the Württemberg general staff on May 11: "If Germany attains her national goal in the nineteenth century, that will seem to me a great achievement, and if it does so in ten or five years, that will be extraordinary, an unexpected gift of a gracious God."

At any rate both Paris and Vienna were now exercising a strong and combined, though different, pressure upon the German national movement, accompanied by sabre-rattling and rumors of war. Only the people of Germany indisposed to bear grudges have long forgotten in what a tense European situation those enthusiastic speeches in favor of national unity were once delivered in the customs parliament. For a moment Napoleon had engaged the opposition at home by stirring up sentiment, but such means can never be employed with impunity, and who could know whether some day the Emperor might not have difficulty in shaking off the very spirits which he had now invoked? However that may be, the successful experiment of April, 1868, probably seemed sufficient encouragement to him to try after several months to start serious negotiations looking toward an alliance with Austria.

Early in July, 1868, Napoleon expressed his regret to Prince Metternich that he had thus far failed to arrive at an agreement with a definite objective, i. e. a treaty providing for a joint plan of action. When the ambassador assured him of Austria's good will, carefully indicating her pacific intentions, however, the Emperor went a step farther and on July 20 asked him the following precise questions, viz. whether a Franco-Austrian entente "for a common, specific purpose" (in other words an "active alliance") were possible, and if not, whether it would be possible to arrange an entente to convoke a European congress so as to insure the present *status quo* of Europe (in other words a "passive alliance"). With these alternatives Napoleon began the negotiations which lasted almost one and one-half years with short interruptions and which by virtue of their informal but morally binding results overlapped with the antecedents of the war of 1870–1871. It was an action which revealed diplomatic reserve on Austria's part from beginning to end while the driving power as well as the clearly defined ambitions and purposes are to be sought on the French side.

Beust rightly interpreted the proposal for an "active alliance" as "a warlike action, at least a joint move having war as its consequence," though France did not *a priori* demand any additional territory but described the restoration of Austrian power in Germany as a satisfactory objective. He realized that the decisions of 1866 could be nullified only by a war, and he knew equally well the secret French designs in case of war on the issue of the Main line. For that very reason he rejected the proposal unconditionally; as in April and in August, 1867—because such an offensive alliance with a non-German power would only serve to estrange the Germans forever from Austria and to consolidate them under Prussia's leadership. To the second proposal he wished to agree only on condition of a surprising modification of the political program. Not a congress for the maintenance of the *status quo*, but a proclamation calling for general disarmament was, he said, the splendid card which none could play better than Napoleon. Let the latter take the initiative before the eyes of Europe in lightening the burden of armaments weighing on France and Europe and, by using his great prestige and moderation, in extending an offer of disarmament, not only materially but also morally, politically and diplomatically. A tempting prospect indeed: the Emperor of the French as the champion of the general yearning for peace, and at the same time as the wise guardian of French interests, the leader in a popular step aiming at the paralysis of Prussian expansion in Germany. In this sense Prince Metternich on August 19 explained to the Emperor that Beust's proposal was preferable to that of a congress, which would seem to the Germans only an intolerable instrument of interference. The idea of disarmament, he argued, would electrify public opinion; it would show the North Germans a means of ridding themselves of their oppressive burdens and would make it possible for the South Germans to escape compulsory military service according to the Prussian model; the leader in such a cause would be a popular idol, while any opponent would incur the hostility of public opinion. It is clear that Beust, who refused to enter a war against Germany on Napoleon's side, sought to attain the same goal in a peaceful diplomatic way, by a sly intervention from within, which was to halt the progressive political and military transformation of Germany and perpetuate its existing unfinished state. This is one of the first examples of the indirect method of diplomatic offensive which the powers of this world have learned to use for the sake of enlisting even the idea of international peace in the service of their selfish interests.

Despite his disappointment over another rejection of his more extensive plans, Napoleon was too shrewd a schemer to overlook the advantages of this counterproposal, though he did not suppress the fear that disarmament might possibly become a trap for him with respect to Prussia and compromise him in the eyes of his own nation. It is characteristic that the emperor, who had just strengthened his army considerably, suggested to his prospective partner not to do anything before the Austrian army act—which, incidentally, was a presupposition of Beust's own pacificism—had been voted in November, but meanwhile to have the whole plan carefully but secretly scrutinized and elucidated by Minister Rouher. After his first conference with the latter the optimistic ambassador saw fit to wire his chief the words: "You are victorious all along the line." But matters after all, did not proceed as quickly.

When on September 14 the Emperor returned

from Châlons to interview Metternich it became obvious that his doubts had increased rather than diminished in the military atmosphere of the camp. His fear that he might, in advocating disarmament, play *un métier de dupe* rested on two considerations. In the first place, he believed that in view of the divergent military systems of France and Prussia a reduction of the peace forces alone would not achieve its purpose; it would be necessary to devise some method to change the very nature of the Prussian system. In the second place, he had the uncomfortable feeling that the opposition, the press and the pacifists might, once he had proposed disarmament, take him at his word and trap him. And so his utterances sounded even more dilatory than before, but he kept urging that the Austrian army act would first have to be passed, saying to the Austrians: "Before talking of disarmament one must be armed, and you are not." Above all he stressed the fact that only positive disarmament could be considered, the conditions of which Rouher was to examine in detail and at his leisure. The ambassador did not try to conceal his disappointment, the less so because he noticed that the Emperor was seeking to revert to the *status quo* as the basis for the treaty as already suggested by him, and Rouher made clear his desire that Austria should, after a speedy completion of her army program "either by means of peace or war," win back her important position in the European balance.

But Beust did not abandon his hope of winning the Emperor over and sought to paint in glowing colors the eloquent manifesto in which the idea of disarmament was to be presented to the peoples of Europe. By such language, he argued, Napoleon would not only create a favorable atmosphere for the elections at home, but would also find sympathy abroad, take the liberals by storm and above all confront Prussia with an embarrassing dilemma. Either Prussia would refuse, in which case Napoleon would have put his antagonist entirely in the wrong while he himself would remain master of the situation with the choice of peace or war; and the responsibility for war or for the continuation of the condition of armed peace would fall upon King William, who would be branded by Europe as the aggressor and would be charged by his own people with having made peace impossible. Or if Prussia consented, and bound itself not to violate the Treaty of Prague in the future, she would cease to be formidable, her prestige among the German nationalists would wane and South Germany would no longer hesitate to organize itself independently. In this situation France could calmly stand by, beginning her own disarmament only after the requisite guarantees had been given. In other words, France "had everything to gain and nothing to lose" in this game. "If France must declare war, she will have public opinion on her side, and if peace is preserved, France will get the chief credit without having made any sacrifices." The Austrian statesman had allowed himself to be moved so far from his peaceful standpoint that at times he even spoke the language of his warlike partner and made suggestion after suggestion which Napoleon might use if he wished for the purpose of humbling Prussia in Germany morally and politically, or of making war upon it with the approval of public opinion. His sanguine assistant, Count Vitzthum, thought he could already foresee the probable outcome of the matter: a lull of a few months pending the passage of the Austrian army act, then in December the initiation of the diplomatic action, and finally, if diplomacy should fail to halt the storm, "the beginning of the military action in February or March, 1869."

And indeed Rouher's plan of September 24 for "an effective and serious disarmament" could be interpreted only as the prelude of an action which, after some introductory words of peace, was bound soon to lead to war. The French proposal provided for disarmament, not forever, but—shrewdly, it seemed—only for a period of ten years. Prussia and France were to bind themselves for this period to reduce their peace footing in each case to 250,000, on condition that Prussia should also agree "to send its reserves home and free them of every military obligation." In other words Prussia was to abolish its entire military system and indeed introduce in the North German Reichstag a bill providing for the abolition of compulsory military service. If in addition to this step, which, it was hoped, would fill the population of the annexed territories with joy Prussia were to abolish also its Landwehr (which would have died a natural death as a result of the abolition of the reserves), France in turn would discontinue the development of the national mobile guard. But even that was not the end of the French desires. Together with these military agreements, Prussia was to assume the obligation not to modify the *status quo* created in Germany by the Treaty of Prague, this *status quo* being interpreted "in a liberating sense for South Germany" (i. e. with dissolution of the treaties of alliance between the North German Confederation and the southern states). Either Prussia would agree, which was not impossible since King William was getting old and might prefer to rest upon his laurels and enjoy ten years of guaranteed peace rather than be exposed to the danger of a war with France or possibly with all of Europe. Or Prussia would refuse. What then? In this more probable event Napoleon would, as Rouher indicated to Count Vitzthum, do what a practical politician would be expected to do before making such sweeping demands upon Prussia. He would probably ask the Austrians what they proposed to do in case of a Prussian refusal. "Are you prepared to support me by armed force in case of necessity?"

The secret machinery and the motives actuating a pseudo-pacifist offensive are rarely so open to view as in this case. The French plan had truly transformed the far from innocuous plan of Beust into something which savored of the "active alliance" which he had rejected. For the concluding query involved nothing less than an attempt to secure in advance and by treaty the military cooperation of Austria in case Prussia turned down the demand for the abolition of its system of compulsory military service and the abandonment of its national mission, a demand which, in all probability would have to be rejected and ought to be rejected. An action which aimed first at the military and then at the political emasculation of the leading German power would certainly have proved only a transitional step on the road to an offensive war in spite of its pacific exterior. Even Beust's plan intended to use the idea of peace only as a decoy, to ruin Prussia's moral standing at home. But the French, in aiming at an alliance with Austria for the purpose of forcing Prussia, in the name of peace and with the threat of war, to abolish its military system—a system which had had its origin in the desire to drive the French invader from German soil—reached the very culmination of hypocrisy. With the olive branch of universal disarmament in her hand, France hoped to confront Prussia and the German nation with the dilemma: either abandon your unity or there will be war.

But apparently the Austrians were not even forced to give an unequivocal answer to this question, which would have been embarrassing for them also. Immediately after the return of the Emperor from Biarritz the entire plan was buried. On October 12, 1868, Lord Clarendon, the future foreign minister of the British Liberals, who were about to assume the reins of government, arrived in Paris. He was favorably disposed to the idea of disarmament like his whole party, and was not averse to a European guarantee of the *status quo*. From Berlin he brought reassuring personal impressions of King William's peaceful disposition. But when Napoleon tried to sound out his old friend, on his (Napoleon's) plan for disarmament—apparently without revealing its basic motives—he met with lively and unconditional opposition.

In this case the Englishman, in spite of his partiality for all peace moves, had enough insight to predict that the plan would serve only to make war inevitable. It seems too that the pretext of security with which Napoleon sought to justify the action of "menaced France," made no impression upon Lord Clarendon. When a few weeks later, after the formation of the liberal ministry in England, the new prime minister Gladstone received the North German ambassador Count Bernstorff, he criticised sharply "the bad traditional policy of the French which always demanded that France be surrounded only by weak states." By this policy, he said, the French merely depreciated themselves "because by virtue of their excellent geographical position, the homogeneity of their population, the wealth of their soil, and the military spirit of their people, they were well able to defend themselves against all attacks and consequently had nothing to fear." [23]

The protest of Clarendon, who as English foreign minister would have been an important figure in the scheme, served Napoleon as a not unwelcome motive for abandoning it. Perhaps he had never entirely given up his inner aversion to a plan which since the advent of the Spanish revolution (immediately described by Bismarck as a drawing-plaster conducive to peace) must have seemed more inopportune than ever. As Metternich soon learned, even the word "disarmament" could now no longer be used in Paris. So much the more important was it for Napoleon not to lose contact with Austria and to draw her still closer to him. The real nature of the pseudo-pacifist episode appears from the fact that it did not end in the peaceful guarantee plans of the English, but rather that after its failure it was secretly merged in a plan for an alliance in which not disarmament and public opinion but armaments and high politics with definite war aims, cloaked in the usual rhetorical phrases, were the chief factors.

VII

As soon as the plan for disarmament fell through, Napoleon thought of another way. He seized upon the idea of a triple alliance between France, Austria and Italy. Only through the cooperation of Italy would Austria be protected in the south and enabled to carry out an ambitious policy such as Napoleon had in mind. To be sure, the new combination would depend upon the satisfaction of Italy's hopes for the Trentino by Austria. But even the first feelers tactfully advanced by the Emperor in his expert way were not absolutely rejected in Vienna. When the Austrian ambassador, referring to the passage of the army act, presented the Emperor with a private memorial on the possibility of a closer understanding, Napoleon agreed with him that the time had come to knit the bonds between the two powers more closely.

On the new basis the secret preliminary conversations began on December 1. Metternich, constantly in touch with Beust, at first conducted them with the Emperor as a private individual and not in his capacity as ambassador. They involved all basic questions pertaining to an alliance. When an understanding had been reached, the official negotiations were started on March 1, 1869, between Paris, Vienna and Florence. With the greatest effort, the draft of a treaty, dated May 10, 1869, was finally agreed upon. With this achievement to its credit, the Napoleonic policy left behind the fitful gropings, which had characterized it since April, 1867, and entered upon a more conclusive stage.

Even after the conclusion of the formally private preliminary conversations, the negotiations were conducted with unusual privacy. On the French side, apart from the Emperor, only Rouher and the new foreign minister La Valette took part in the negotiations. The men who had advocated conciliation of Prussia in 1866 were now the leaders in the offensive policy of isolating Prussia, whereas even the Duc de Gramont, formerly the bearer of secret offers of alliance, was not let into the secret during the entire tenure of his office as ambassador in Vienna. Since the seat of the negotiations was in Paris, it is obvious, especially in view of the personal conduct of affairs by Napoleon, that the reports of Metternich and Vitzthum are the decisive source for these matters, while the files of the French ministry may be expected to contain much less material. Indeed Paris has boasted on more than one important occasion that certain events would leave no traces behind in the archives. The "secrets of Paris" are now all in Vienna, and the Austrian records, though not complete, are full enough [1] not only to lift the veil from the surface of the diplomatic proceedings, but also to uncover the deeper motives and aims which are the decisive factors in any estimate of Napoleon's policy.

For it was Napoleon who, as Beust later empha-

---

[1] To be sure Beust and Vitzthum burned a part of their secret correspondence in November, 1871, and since the archives of the Austrian embassy in Paris were later destroyed by fire, the gaps cannot be filled by reference to the embassy collection. Still a goodly share of the private correspondence of Metternich and Vitzthum is preserved in the state archives. It will probably take some time before the continuation of the *Origines diplomatiques de la guerre de 1870–1871* reaches these negotiations. But much more light would probably be thrown on the course of events by the publication of the Italian secret documents. It is to be hoped that the present work will prove an incentive for their publication.

nized strongly, had the initiative and leadership in his hand. The Austrian and Italian negotiators were always more prepared to lend ears to his plans and ideas than the cabinets of Vienna and Florence deemed desirable. More than once we see Metternich under the influence of the Emperor exceeding the instructions sent him by Beust, so that the Emperor Francis Joseph expressed the hope as early as December 9, 1869, that "Beust's instructions would induce the ambassador to abandon his dangerous deviations and his excessive compliance to the wishes of Napoleon and lead him back to the right course." It is characteristic of Napoleon's ultimate aims that in one of his very first conversations with Metternich he added to his offers the carefully considered observation: If France and Austria should ever have to undertake a joint military action, no matter how far off that time might be, it would be very important to come to an understanding on military matters, i. e., the strategic question would have to be discussed betimes and not postponed until it is too late for mature consideration.[24] As soon as Paris perceived that scruples were arising in Vienna on the riskiness of the adventure, an effort was made to screw up Austria's courage as much as possible. When for example some rumors leaked out, in spite of all caution and secrecy, when Bismarck in parliamentary addresses began to allude to a conspiracy and launched newspaper attacks against Beust's policies, operating with heavy ammunition, as was his wont, against a hidden powder magazine, Napoleon on January 14, 1869, took these attacks as a pretext to make a formal declaration in Vienna, almost in the manner of a protector, and stated that France would not permit Prussia to commit any overt acts against Austria. Thenceforth Vienna could rely upon the unconditional determination of France to take the offensive.

But if this offensive will was to attain its goal, it was bound, in the course of the negotiations—which can not here be analysed in detail—to adjust itself to the viewpoint of the other side as much as possible. First of all Paris had to content itself with letting Beust make the more favorable Near Eastern question, instead of the unsuitable German question, the starting point. In this way it would be possible gradually to transform the passive alliance into an active one. In the same way Paris adopted Beust's view that a joint policy in the German question, instead of injuring the national sensibilities by premature intervention, could be carried out successfully only by an exercise of restraint. But having made such concessions, the diplomatic efforts of France were bent more than ever upon defining more precisely Austria's practical obligation in case of war. Again and again France tried to strike out of the treaty the neutrality clause demanded by Austria for the event of a localized Franco-Prussian conflict, and tried her best to secure at least a contractual assurance that in this case Austria would begin to arm and station an observation corps in Bohemia. But in all essential points Beust's shrewd maneuvering policy was successful. He was interested far more in securing for Austria a permanent position as a great power than he was in preparing any special action.

It is not surprising therefore that the negotiators from the three camps had to travel a laborious road before they could agree on May 10 to the draft of a treaty. In truth it was like the task of Penelope, for the formula agreed upon one day would have to be given up, almost over night, in favor of a new one. If Vitzthum occasionally felt like the skipper in the fable, who had to take the goat and the cabbage across the river, it seems that the old story of the wolf, the goat and the cabbage fits the situation even better. For the difficulties were not limited to the material claims which had to be adjusted, they extended even to the external form and included the question whether there was to be a single treaty or several different treaties. These difficulties showed again and again that despite the common interests, the foreign and domestic policies of the three parties rested upon distinctly divergent promises.

The main treaty only laid down the great principles, viz. a joint policy of the three powers in Europe; reciprocal guarantee of each other's territory; in case of war conclusion of a defensive and offensive alliance, the conditions of which were reserved to a special convention; after the war joint settlement of all questions of compensation and territorial readjustment. A protocol worked out at the same time contained an agreement on the proper measures to be carried out in the event of war. The Italians, in return for concessions specified in detail, agreed to raise an army of 200,000 as soon as one of the contracting parties was attacked. The decisive article read: "If Austria is unexpectedly attacked by Prussia, or if for any other reason war should break out between Austria and Prussia, France and Italy assume the obligation to take part in the war immediately and to support Austria with all their military forces in order to maintain her territorial integrity."

The nature of the compensations and readjustments was not stated in the treaty itself, for diplomatic documents generally say the least about the motives and aims of the contracting parties. At any rate the German program of Napoleon, which was the hidden war objective in this triple alliance, appears with undeniable certainty from the negotiations.

One phase of the program was revealed by Count Vitzthum as early as February 19. Both powers agreed not to lay down their arms in case of war until there has been created in Germany a new confederation consisting of states as nearly as possible of the same strength, this being the objective in the war.[25] Similar formulas occur in the various drafts and finally too in the war aims which were confidentially communicated by Paris to a third power in August, 1870. There could be no question what this harmless formula was to mean for Germany's future. It aimed at the dismemberment of Prussia and its reduction to the size and importance of Bavaria and Saxony; a division of power in Germany whereby one element would neutralize the other and admit neither of combination nor of leadership. While Napoleon had formerly tried to unify North Germany under Prussian leadership in conformity with his nationalist policy, after being keenly disappointed in not receiving his broker's fee he now returned to the old favorite dream of his nation, to the ideal of a Germany of

1648, which was to appeal even to the French of 1919 as the only real form of good neighborly organization.

In any case such an organization of Germany assured the French of their second and foremost war objective, the Rhine. Of course the Rhine was never mentioned, not even in the first drafts, because Beust still adhered to the principle of not binding himself expressly and in advance in this respect and instructed his ambassador repeatedly to avoid everything in the text which might disturb the sensibilities of the Hungarians and the "sentimentality" of the German Austrians. And so we find Prince Metternich reporting on March 1, 1869, with unconcealed irony: "The Teutons for their part will not find the Rhine mentioned in the text, a thing which I achieved not without difficulty. They will not be able to raise a cry about a joint warlike enterprise by us and the foreigner against 'their German brothers.' "[26] It seems that the French, as in the case of their previous frank offers, wished to have their real goal mentioned in the treaty, but they had to yield. Chaste ears must not hear what chaste hearts cannot spare. Up to the very outbreak of the war in 1870 Beust had to emphasize to his hot-headed ally again and again that he must not betray any designs against German territory and must not unnecessarily excite the national sensibilities of the Germans.

But in other connections the offensive will of the alliance is not so carefully veiled as in the text. It appears clearly in the conditions which France and Austria had to grant their other partner, for this subsidiary power succeeded in submitting an insatiable bill of desiderata in return for the 200,000 men whom it was to station along the Rhine. The conditions included South Tyrol and in an extreme case the Isonzo line as well; Nice; Tunis (an advance notice for the future); Ticino, in case Switzerland should not maintain its neutrality (a claim reserved for later days); a loan and a promise of compensation to cover the war costs; a joint policy with regard to the Vatican Council and papal election; establishment of a *modus vivendi* with the papal state —all that and even more was sought by the Italians! It is not surprising that during the days of the agreement the skilful Italian representative Count Vimercati smilingly admitted to Count Vitzthum: "La Valette says that this treaty is peace . . . Well, war is not knocking at the door, but Napoleon would never have proposed such a treaty to us if he did not have the fixed idea of using his armies." What is more, the liberality with which the French satisfied the appetite of a power not directly interested in the war aims of the other, throws light upon the war price which—in addition to the Balkanization of Germany—they expected to exact for themselves and refrained from mentioning in the treaty only because of the insistence of their Austrian partner.

The real significance of the negotiations lies in the fact that the French policy of preventing the unification of Germany,—not only the previous passive policy of the Main line, but also the whole complex of far-reaching positive incursions—was to be protected and reinforced by a system of European alliances. To be sure the success of the endeavor would have meant a new order, a fundamental event, which would have served as a criterion for European politics as a whole. In this sense the Austrian plenipotentiary Count Vitzthum was right in saying that nothing since the Holy Alliance had introduced a conception even remotely resembling this in general significance, that for the first time a new political system had been established in Europe and that the Triple Alliance of the three monarchs who ruled over 100 million people and disposed of almost three million bayonets would take the place of the League of the Eastern Powers, and that by virtue of the identity of faith, of internal dangers and joint interests in the east as well as in the west it guaranteed this political and geographical trinity and was worthy of the best traditions of a Kaunitz. This rhetoric was characteristic of the Austrian point of view, which always stressed the idea of defence and the applicability of the alliance to the Near East. The French viewpoint, which had long since relegated Near Eastern interests to the background, saw in this new grouping the aggressive instrument of a policy of intervention, which it was hoped could be used in due time to achieve an object long aimed at by various methods.

Only against the background of this encirclement of 1869 with its extreme danger for the German body politic, which was just in a transitional state of development, does the policy of Bismarck appear in its true setting. It has often been characterized as a policy of "blood and iron," although the phrase was intended to apply only to a trial of strength between German powers and never to a trial with foreign states. In other words it applied to a conflict which was as inevitable for the achievement of German unity as was the similar struggle, simultaneously raging in the United States, for the preservation of American national unity. It has been overlooked by the opponents of Bismarck's policy that after the decision of Königgrätz this policy was inspired by a deep sense of responsibility for the peace of Europe and maintained a predominantly defensive attitude. In fact, from the summer of 1867 on it was more and more forced into the defensive by its opponents. The German historians too have often been guided by the false assumption that because this policy was crowned with success in 1870–1871, it had a definite objective in view from the very start and pursued it with an air of Machiavellian superiority. In contrast to the bright progress towards victory the dangers encountered by Bismarck's policy are left too much in obscurity, whereas they should be recognized as realities and thrown into high relief. For this reason nothing is more absurd than to look upon Bismarck as the new Machiavelli, endowed with diabolical arts and surrounded by innocent, unsuspecting contemporaries who despised "blood and iron," when in reality he had as his opponents a Napoleon, a Beust and a Victor Emmanuel. A policy of might is common to all states. But Napoleon's policy was reprehensible and was prepared at all times to interfere in the sphere of national interest of another state, while Bismarck's policy, without infringing upon the vital national interests of others, constantly restricted itself to the problem of gradually satisfying the urge of the German nation for unification, without seriously endangering peace. If, in the face of a policy of encirclement which threatened some day to stifle Germany's future, he sought counter-weights in Europe and got in touch with

Hungarian elements, who were on their own account opposed to an active German policy on the part of the Viennese cabinet, he had a right to do so. And if finally he included in his calculations the efforts of the Spanish to win over the Archduke Leopold of Hohenzollern, he was again merely doing his duty and exercising the right of self-defence. Of course it can not be denied that this candidacy was meant to be a counter-balance. And it is just as certain that in comparison with the weighty, serious reality of the Triple Alliance it was as light and insignificant as a feather; at the decisive moment it proved an illusion, the substance of which was to burst like a bubble. Hence there is no justification for condemning this act of Bismarck (as has frequently been done, most recently by an American) because it was bound to "offend" France. As if the United States had a short time before hesitated to "offend" the daredevil policy of Napoleon in Mexico and inflict upon it a defeat which in world history has the same significance as the thunderclap of Sadowa had in continental Europe! Why should Bismarck have been considerate in view of this conspiracy led by Napoleon, which, had it been successful, would have hurled Germany back into the darkest ages of internal dissolution and external dependence?

Naturally even he could not yet foresee all the dangers, but it was his foremost duty to meet the eventualities which his political instinct sensed. Rifle in hand, he fulfilled his duty without a formal challenge, and without overstepping the line of watchful waiting which he had drawn at the time of the customs parliament in May, 1868. As the dark clouds were already gathering and the rumors of war growing apace, he declared on February 19, 1869, in his instructions to the North German representative in Paris that he did not fear war and that the threatening reports in various forms had come from Paris again and again since the summer of 1866: "In the face of all this we can do naught but trust in our strength and remain calm, so that beyond the Rhine too the impression will gain ground that we can not be intimidated." Toward the end of March he had representations made to the Italian government because it did not officially deny the rumors of a triple alliance. Thereupon the Italian minister read to him a private letter of the Premier General Menabrea, who described France as a fully charged battery which was bound to explode at the slightest contact. He said that it was incumbent upon Prussia carefully to avoid every such contact and circumvent the conflict, and to do its best to satisfy and disinterest France. Bismarck was right in replying to this ambiguous advice that it seemed to him that Paris rather than Berlin was the right address for petitions in the interest of conciliation and peace, and that Germany's defensive strength was the only means of disinteresting France. What made Bismarck so sure of himself was not only his realization of the irreconcilability of interests which stood in the way of a final union of his opponents but also his deep conviction that he was representing the cause of the future, the unity of a great nation, transcending all intrigues and contingencies.

Already Vienna was instructing Prince Metternich to agree formally in the name of the Emperor to the treaty of May 10. Only the question of formal procedure—whether it was to be signed by the plenipotentiaries or by the sovereigns, with the counter-signatures of the ministers,—was still undecided. Already Beust was declaring that he now considered Napoleon to be morally bound and that he looked upon Austria as the ally of France. And then difficulties set in which delayed the formal settlement, so that Napoleon was finally enabled to bring only part of the harvest, without the external form and full content of the treaties, under cover.

On the one hand the Italians tried to raise the price at the eleventh hour. Not only did they demand the Isonzo line of the Austrians at the last minute, but they availed themselves also of the instrument of parliamentary obstruction to introduce for the first time the question of the evacuation of Rome, and this was a more serious matter. A second cause for delay was furnished by the conditions in France, which had been changed since the elections of May 23. To be sure, Rouher, despite the unfavorable outcome of the Paris elections, declared to the Austrian ambassador optimistically and coolly, as was his wont, that the Emperor would remain firm, and that on the day when he might wish to make war France and even Paris would follow him. But the riots which took place in Paris from June 8 to 13 seemed proof enough that Napoleon's throne was no longer firm. The composition of the new chambers too left hardly a doubt that the personal, absolutist regimes had suffered a serious blow. It was at this time that the Austrian military attaché declared that it was doubtful whether the Emperor could distract the country by war even if he wished.

Napoleon was not willing to be halted. He stated to Prince Metternich on June 25, as the latter was leaving for Ischl to see his Emperor with regard to the difficulties which had arisen: "I shall look upon this treaty as already signed." [27] He threw his whole personal authority into the balance to promote the treaties which his subjects were already beginning to criticise and which were meeting opposition in the new legislature. On the other hand, the Italians considered the moment ripe for exploiting the crisis in France in their own interest and for demanding, early in July, the formal evacuation of Rome and non-intervention in the Roman question, as conditions for their signature of the treaty. If in addition they demanded a promise that nothing be done against German unity, this was apparently nothing more than a gross attempt at extortion, with a view to attaining their real desiderata.

Such was the situation which Metternich found upon his return to Paris on July 14. The negotiations had been tied up, Rouher and La Valette had retired before the attacks of the chambers, new leaders had taken over the reins, and there was new cause for delay. It was a decisive crisis, such as the Empire had never experienced before. It reached its climax when on August 20 Napoleon, perhaps as a result of the excitement, got a serious attack of bladder trouble and for weeks—as had been the case also in July, 1866—disappeared entirely as a factor in a state the very basis of which was his name and sole authority. Naturally after this experience public opinion in France, carried away by exaggerated rumors, became convinced that the personal regime, weakened by a chain of reverses at home and abroad, was nearing its end. The Italians tried all the more eagerly to utilize this critical condition for their Roman ambitions. They took the course leading through Vienna, in order to exercise pressure on Paris, and apparently they did not shun indiscretions with respect to the negotiations, hoping in this way perhaps to exercise an influence upon the decisions of the weakening Emperor. But these very indiscretions had an unexpected result in that they led to English intervention in Paris, comparable in a way to the intervention of the autumn of 1868. Lord Clarendon was all the more wrought up over these rumors because he was just working upon his favorite plan for general disarmament as a guarantee of peace. He appeared on September 18 before the convalescing French Emperor and, in connection with his disarmament plans, submitted to him the serious question what the meaning of this triple alliance was. Napoleon calmly denied everything. "I admitted nothing," he declared to his intimates. He assured him that the entente had no warlike or secret purpose and that there had merely been pourparlers, which had proved unsuccessful.

Nevertheless the Emperor was henceforth compelled to exercise great caution. And so he decided to get out of the still pending negotiations everything he could without yielding to Italy and without compromising himself in the eyes of England. That meant the renunciation of formal signatures to the treaties for the present, but at the same time getting an equivalent therefore in the shape of an exchange of letters by the rulers themselves, this being the only substitute, of the many suggested by Vienna and Florence, which would establish a moral obligation of equal political force.

In his letter to Emperor Francis Joseph of September 24 Napoleon stated that if Austria were threatened, he would without hesitation stand by her side with all the strength at his command. He promised further not to negotiate with any power without previous consultation with Austria, and said that he was ready to agree to a written confirmaticn of the entente with Italy, despite the danger of Italian indiscretion, if Francis Joseph should insist. Of the answer of Francis Joseph nothing is known except that it too made the promise not to enter any negotiations without previously informing Napoleon, but that it did not reciprocate the voluntary promise of aid on Napoleon's part. So far as Italy was concerned, all further steps were left to Napoleon's discretion. A letter of Victor Emmanuel to Napoleon warmly supported the aims of the alliance but again stressed the necessity of evacuating Rome. The significance of these letters lay in the fact that they obligated the writers morally in the sense of the unsigned treaty. This was repeatedly recognized by all three parties—by Italy, to be sure, with the Roman reservation. To his confidant Rouher, Napoleon in October described the situation created by the letters as follows: "I consider our treaties as morally signed. The alliance with Austria is the corner-stone of my policy." [28] He believed that he had Austria firmly in his hand, and this idea, though associated in his mind with certain illusions, played a decisive rôle even in the decisions of July, 1870. And Italy he hoped he could use in due time, as soon as he was ready to pay the price—perhaps even without paying it.

In this way the Emperor believed he had insured the essence of his foreign policy against all eventualities of the parliamentary form of Government, which had arisen as the new French form of government in consequence of the crisis of the past few months. Even while this transition was still taking place under the greatest general tension, he informed the Austrians that no matter what happened he would remain his own minister of war and his own foreign minister. And indeed, while Napoleon was still secretly negotiating with Emile Ollivier, the man of the people and of peace, concerning his participation in the ministry, he was just as secretly at work placing another iron into the fire. In the course of November he summoned General Lebrun to discuss with him the necessity of evolving a plan of campaign. When the general declared that this would be possible only if one knew who the allies were to be, the Emperor replied: "It is permissible to regard the alliance with Italy as certain and that with Austria as morally if not actually assured." [29] It would seem as if this had been the cue, for it is no accident that even before Christmas—we do not know whence the initiative came—Archduke Albrecht planned a trip to France. The purpose of this trip was to initiate what Napoleon had even before the beginning of the treaty negotiations described as necessary, namely an understanding on strategic questions in case of war.

The Empire was entering upon a new form of government. But the imperial gambler, hiding behind the confused front wings of the parliamentary experiment, was secretly continuing to spin the threads which were to weave the fate of his dynasty and the destiny of France into a permanent woof. It was characteristic of his brooding, speculative nature that he did not speak the last word, but kept it to himself. He was not the man to proceed straightway toward his goal. There was something in his nature which partook of the spirit of Schiller's Wallenstein. Like Wallenstein he pursued no decided course, was slow in making decisions, but liked to dally with ideas, and allow himself to be carried away by the desire for freedom of action and by the lust for power. And so he continued in his attempt to create the circumstances which would lead him to the goal of his dreams, but the question was whether, when the time seemed ripe to others, he would still possess the freedom of action necessary for making the ultimate decisions.

VIII

WITH the beginning of the parliamentary regime in France in January, 1870, history is compelled more than before to distinguish between the foreground and the background of political life. From this time until the plebiscite of May 8, 1870, which closed the parliamentary episode in the narrower sense, we can detect in the French foreign policy various lines, apparently disconnected and yet shrewdly held together, running parallel with one another.

The parliamentary era was opened with words of peace and with a pretence of disarmament. If we would judge it, we must above all remember the important fact that neither Premier Ollivier, who at least had the reputation of being a pacifist, nor the new foreign minister Daru, who, it was generally believed, was under the influence of Thiers, were initiated by Napoleon into the secrets of the negotiations of 1869 and their results. While the Emperor sought to give more depth to the moral ententes, the ministers proceeded on their course without knowledge of the real foreign policy of France and confident of their parliamentary position, speaking the language of peace and of liberal reforms. But even in this a new note could be detected when Daru, like his predecessors, emphasized that he would recognize the situation created by the Treaty of Prague but would tolerate no transgression of the conditions of peace. At the least violation of its provisions, the irritable and self-willed man declared to the world, he would go to the legislature and ascend the tribune; at the least irritation of her skin France would start up from her sleep. The fact is that this youthful parliamentarism possessed, with regard to foreign methods, a double bottom. On the one hand, in contrast to the former personal regime and its uncertainties, it was heralded as a new and reliable guarantee of peace and as such commended to German public opinion. On the other hand, it served as the instrument of those currents which since the summer of 1866 tended more and more in one direction, and the minister in his parliamentary pride was determined to use these means to the full in order to lend a semblance of popular sanction to his language. It was a question whether this did not give chauvinism a still more incalculable instrument, which after long suppression might become even a greater menace to peace than the lonely broodings of the Emperor.

And if we analyse the actual facts, this seems to be true of the move for disarmament in which Napoleon succeeded in interesting Lord Clarendon. The latter, up to this time a disinterested champion of European peace, now got into a predicament which is likely to confront any honest mediator. Believing in the purity of the motives of the one party—and the new parliamentary form of the Ollivier ministry seemed to Lord Clarendon the safest possible guarantee of peace and liberty—, he attempts to influence the other party, but in doing so he acts unconsciously as the agent of the secret motives of that first party. While making personal and private suggestions in Berlin, from January 1870 on, Lord Clarendon, apparently acting on his own initiative and in strict confidence, was almost certainly in touch with Paris and was being victimized by the French wire-pullers. In France the contingent of recruits for 1870 had been reduced by 10,000 as a visible evidence of the French love for peace and as a symbol of the new era. Metternich privately characterized this measure as ridiculous, and in fact it had no significance at all because the full quota had never been approached in the drafts. Its sole purpose was to serve as a background for Clarendon's action (he himself did not appreciate its significance), in order to prove to Berlin that the intentions of France were good, and to discredit the King of Prussia in the eyes of the mediator in case he refused.

At the same time the question of disarmament was cautiously presented to public opinion. Since a peace move initiated by England met with some approval even in the legislatures of the individual German states, it was possible, as Beust had already suggested in the fall of 1868, to offer to an anti-Prussian opposition high-sounding pacifist arguments, without letting the inexperienced German politicians guess who was pulling the wires in these schemes to frustrate Bismarck's policy. The next step then was secretly to undermine the defensive and offensive alliances uniting North and South Germany. The attacks of the particularist opposition in Bavaria against the Hohenlohe ministry, centering around the question of the *casus foederis*, were welcomed by the French as a promising prelude. Thus a new particularism, which really owed its existence to the European situation, began to play into the hands of the French, in part consciously but in the great majority of cases quite unwittingly. What weeds it is possible to sow on such a field is shown by an article in the "Bayrisches Vaterland" of February 9, 1870, which during the Hohenlohe crisis made the patriotic utterance that the treaties of 1866 would be observed as long as possible, for instance until the French were in Schwabing or the Austrians in Sendling. Shortsightedly the only effective guarantee which Germany had against the outside world was assailed, while Napoleon proceeded, without paying any attention to the pacifist gestures of his ministers, to strengthen the morally binding entente with Austria by military agreements.

The attitude of the parliamentary ministers toward German unity was now more arrogant than before, despite all their assurances of peace. When a national liberal member of the North German Reichstag (Lasker) very inopportunely moved that Baden be admitted into the North German Confederation, Bismarck in a statesmanlike address opposed the motion for internal as well as external reasons. He steadfastly refused to exercise any pressure upon the South Germans, although he interjected the remark that he considered the unification of Germany an incontestable right of the nation, in case the South German states should voluntarily make the suggestion. Count Daru expressed to the North German ambassador his approval of Bismarck's declaration, so far as it referred to the present, but at the same time, in a schoolmaster's tone, he volunteered the advice to postpone the question of German unification to the Greek calends. It seems to have escaped the German pacifists to this very day that this was the underlying motive of the French policy and its talk of disarmament. It is quite comprehensible, then, that Metternich should have declared in March that no French minister had yet taken so strong a stand against Prussia as had Daru.

It is very instructive to see in the reports of the Austrian ambassador the reflection of the true sentiment of the court and leaders of France in this new era. It is not surprising to find Rouher, driven from power but still enjoying the confidence of Napoleon, trying to assure the ambassador that as soon as the Austrians wanted to go to war the Emperor would join them, and saying that the Emperor was coming around to the view that a good foreign war at the right time would be of the greatest service to him. He seemed to the Austrian to be wrapped up in the idea of striking a decisive blow in the form of a declaration of war against Prussia. It was still more significant at this moment that Thiers too, who was looked upon as the real adviser of Daru and for this reason was frequently visited by the ambassador, showed himself to be quite in agreement with this conception of the situation. Metternich thought he was justified in concluding from these conversations that Rouher as well as Thiers, should either come to power, would plan a war and take the Rhine, the former for the purpose of restoring the authoritative government of December 2, the latter in the interest of his own fame and name in history.[30] The impression which Thiers' attitude made upon Metternich was so strong that he went to the Emperor and made a report to him (a thing which Thiers had expected from the beginning). Napoleon's answer was: "If M. Thiers is really for war, under certain conditions, I should despise him less." [31] It was like lifting the veil a bit from his inmost soul. The republican opposition presented a not dissimilar picture, for its characteristically peaceful sentiments were intermingled with some rather martial strains. In the preceding year Vitzthum had already uttered his opinion of the peace sermons of the opposition. He said that the latter feared only a strengthening of the imperial prestige as a result of a Napoleonic victory, and that it desired a war for the republic, which would have a chance to subsist only after having given the army an opportunity to get revenge for Sadowa. Now in March, 1870, the republican deputy Bethmont confessed to the Austrian ambassador that he longed to show what a free France could do, if she should ever have the good fortune to march hand in hand with Austria. Hence Metternich concluded: "That is the republican, who like Rouher, the absolutist, and Thiers, the parliamentarian, thinks with pleasure of a war at our side. I know very well, the Rhine is the great enchanter of the nation—our fair eyes have little to do with it. Another reason for joining our aims inseparably with theirs when one day the trumpet of war resounds." [32] So far as Germany and the Rhine were concerned, all parties were now, just as in the 'thirties and 'forties, guided by the same impulses and headed for the same goal. Their struggle with each other for power compelled them all the more to agree on this one question, and even to outdo each other in order not to be left behind.

The Emperor was conscious of this invisible power behind the throne, indeed he felt he was its chosen instrument. In this spirit he proceeded secretly to reinforce the morally binding arrangements of 1869. Toward the end of February Archduke Albrecht arrived in Paris on the journey which had been prepared long ago and the purpose of which was to discuss confidentially with the Emperor the plans for a joint campaign. The elements of this plan have long been known in detail. The war was to begin with a simultaneous attack against South Germany by the three allies each with 100,000 men, (the Italians concentrating against Munich). Then all the forces were to march in the direction of the line Würzburg—Nürnberg—Amberg.[33] They were to advance according to Napoleon's plans of 1806 and fight the decisive battle at Leipzig, as Thiers' strategy had planned as early as 1866. The peace was to be dictated at Berlin. The success of this plan would have brought about a realization of all the objectives which the diplomats had aimed at in their negotiations of a year ago. The conversations took place in private, to be sure, but during the festivities in honor of the victor of Custozza the French generals showed by their every act, more clearly than the politicians had done, that war was inevitable.

It must be confessed that at first the military conversations between Napoleon and Archduke Albrecht had a purely academic character. It is particularly noteworthy that the military plans were not based upon clear political obligations on the part of Austria, and that very great difficulties confronted these plans because of important underlying difficulties such as the impossibility of mobilizing all three armies at the same rate of speed. What the practical consequences of the first negotiations may have been is another question. In this connection the salient point is that behind the scenes of the parliamentary-pacifist era Napoleon, without the knowledge of his uninitiated ministers Ollivier and Daru, proceeded to strengthen the political bonds by military arrangements which from the beginning he had declared to be necessary for the completion of the alliance. At a later period the correspondence of Grey and Cambon of November, 1912, was supplemented by an exchange of ideas on the part of the general staffs in much the same way. While Lord Clarendon in irenic letters communicated his good advice to Berlin, and while French diplomacy stealthily tried to shoot holes into the *casus foederis* of the treaties of 1866, the military dreams of Napoleon, patterned on those of his uncle and aiming at the destruction of Prussia, now began to assume definite proportions.

The conversations with Archduke Albrecht were only the first step, for after Francis Joseph had given his consent in April they were to be continued in Vienna. But before these additional steps could be taken, Napoleon characteristically enough decided to strengthen his personal position in the parliamentary system and above all to get rid of the obnoxious and conceited Daru, and take the management of foreign affairs in hand personally. The idea of a plebiscite doubtless had its domestic motives, but the decision of the Emperor was recognizably influenced also by the considerations of foreign policy, by the experiences of the past few months, and by his speculations for the future. The plebiscite was in fact associated by initiated persons with a decided turn in the internal and external policies of the empire. Ollivier too, who in the course of these months surrendered more and more to the alluring influence of his monarch, was in favor of this turn. The picture of the man of the people and of peace was already being compared by Metternich with the portrait of a beginner wherein the corrections and bold strokes of a master hand are clearly visible.

The plebiscite of May 8, the vote of confidence at home, and the blow against the purely parliamentary system coincided almost to the hour with the transfer of the foreign ministry to a man who was not distinguished by his ability but was known as an uncompromising advocate of action. It was the Duc de Gramont, the ambassador in Vienna. This change too throws light upon the episodic nature of the parliamentary experiment, marked by a peculiar contrast of soft notes of peace and loud rumblings of war.

IX

THE new course of the empire since the plebiscite is characterized by two simultaneous events occurring under the surface. On the same day (May 18) on which Beust proposed that the new foreign minister Gramont be personally initiated into the negotiations of 1869, a military crown council met in Paris with the Emperor in the chair, in order to decide on the continuation of the military negotiations begun by Archduke Albrecht. Here are two lines of future development, historically connected but outwardly separate and held together only in the person of the Emperor.

The Duc de Gramont was the sixth foreign minister who since the beginning of the German crisis conducted the affairs of France and tried to maintain himself in a transformed world. He combined the sharply anti-Prussian partisanship of Drouyn de Lhuys with the irritable awkwardness of Marquis de Moustier. His personal note, which distinguished him from his predecessors, was a mixture of highfaluting carelessness, irrelevancy and lack of self-control—an extremely dangerous combination for a leader in difficult situations. He was even ready to assume the parliamentary self-assurance of his predecessor Daru, for when Beust, after finally securing permission from Napoleon, initiated the unsuspecting ambassador into the secrets of the treaty drafts on May 27 and of the monarchical letters of 1869, he assumed an air of hurt pride and suggested that the will of the sovereign alone was no longer sufficient. The engagements, he said, would be null and void if he did not assume them. But he was willing to do so. The fact that the French foreign minister, five weeks before the outbreak of war, was in this way initiated into the situation which had already existed for a year and which formed the very cornerstone of Napoleon's policy—that he was initiated by the minister of a foreign, though "morally bound" power—while the French premier Ollivier was still kept out of the secret—this is perhaps unique in history. For a man of his nature it was bound to prove disastrous that after learning of the agreements of 1869 he no longer found time to become thoroughly familiar with the network of reservations with which Beust had surrounded these agreements, and that under the stimulating influence of the thought that he now held in his hand everything which he himself had tried in vain to achieve in 1867–1868, he went to Paris with an exaggerated urge for action, to become minister of foreign affairs.

At the same time General Lebrun went to Vienna at Napoleon's behest. The council of war (Leboeuf, Frossard, Lebrun and Jarras) of May 19, to which Napoleon submitted the strategic plans of Archduke Albrecht on the cooperation of France, Austria, Italy and Denmark, had declared the project feasible only in case the three powers would declare war simultaneously, beginning their mobilization and their military operations at the same time, since only in this way, by a simultaneous advance on the Rhine and Saar, from the direction of Bohemia, from the Brenner and from the North Sea and Baltic, could the enemy be compelled to divide his forces and be prevented from concentrating overwhelming forces on the Rhine and Saar. But since Austria would, according to the Archduke, require six weeks for her mobilization and neither Italy nor Denmark could mobilize more rapidly, the Austrian project appeared inacceptable and seriously misleading. The only man in the council who discounted this suspicious criticism and refused to admit Machiavellian computations "on the part of his allies, especially Austria," was the Emperor himself. As usual he reserved his ultimate opinion and declared only that he would send Lebrun to Vienna for further discussions with the Archduke. Lebrun left Paris on May 27, and after having quietly observed the German forces in Cologne, Berlin and Dresden, arrived in Vienna on June 7. His talks with the Archduke, however, did not alter the military problem materially. Moreover he could not deny that the authentic political sentiment in Vienna remained the same. For Emperor Francis Joseph, to whom the general was presented by the Archduke on June 14 in Laxenburg castle, assured him that he needed peace and made the significant statement: "If I make war, I shall have to be forced into it," explaining this by the words: "When Napoleon stands in South Germany with his army not as an enemy but as a liberator, I for my part shall be compelled to declare that I will make his cause my own." This was a renewed admission of the moral ties and of the common interests, but also a definite expression of the reservation that Austria would defer her participation in the military action until France had achieved a decisive victory. But it seems that Napoleon was more anxious to hear an expression of the spirit of fraternity in arms than the reservations. And so he raised no objection when Lebrun, in his report during the last week of June, called attention to the fact that the very first military demonstrations on the part of Austria, though staged in the guise of neutrality, would be bound to exercise a strong moral influence on Berlin and lead to the reinforcement of the Saxon and Silesian frontiers, and that even further modifications could be made in the plans of the Archduke. Such possibilities occupied the restless mind of the Emperor a few days before the explosion of the Spanish bomb.

Meanwhile the confident Duke of Gramont proceeded on his course of action. Of the threads which he tried to spin in European politics it is possible to detect only a few, yet it is significant that in the German question too he tried to take a more active hand, although there was no special point at issue. The very manner in which he answered the parliamentary interpellation of June 20 on the St. Gotthard railway revealed to diplomatic observers how strongly the chauvinist embers were smouldering under the ashes. On June 25 Gramont told the North German ambassador that an interpellation was pending in the chamber on alleged modifications of the fortifications of Mainz (as a matter of fact only unimportant municipal boundary rectifications were involved). If we remember the rôle which Mainz played in the earlier crises from 1848 on, when Thiers was to acquire the keys of Germany for France, up to the claims for compensation of 1866 and the subterranean plans of the past few years, then this step of Gramont (characterized in a later marginal note of Bismarck as "very impudent") appears in its true light. There seemed even to be system in it, for the minister—though a novice in parliamentary matters—followed up the first step by a second on July 1, announcing to the ambassador that the opposition would discuss German questions during the budget deliberations and appending to this an express reminder of the peace of Prague. He seemed inclined to take the wind of parliamentary sentiments into his sails, though he knew that the signs pointed to storm. When on the same day the debate on the military budget and the reduction of the recruit contingent by 10,000 men took place in the legislature, the Bonapartist hotspur Granier de Cassagnac went so far as to exclaim: "Let us take the Rhine, then we can decrease the army by 100,000. That is the way to cut down the war budget; there is no other." It was the voice of old-time France, the France of Louis XIV and Napoleon I which expressed itself in this shrill cry. Although the diplomacy of Napoleon III had learned to advance silently, its partisans noised their views about without any consideration.

The political atmosphere was heavily charged and if an external cause were to unify the hesitant speculations of the Emperor, the awkward aggressiveness of Gramont and the irritable urge of the parliament for action, the effect could no more be checked than the blind workings of fate which invisibly guide men's footsteps.

X

A FEW days after the events just described, the news that the Spanish government had offered Prince Leopold of Hohenzollern-Sigmaringen the royal crown became known in Paris. Within a few hours the candidacy of the prince begot in the men who controlled the destinies of the state a will for war which was to transform into action the thought with which they had long been toying.

In writing the history of the origins of the war of 1870–1871 critics have usually committed the mistake of detaching the events of July, 1870, too much from the general French policy of the years 1863–1870, and of artificially isolating and reducing to the events of a brief period a problem which can be understood only in relation to its whole environment. An exact philological method which minutely examines the days, hours and minutes of the final tension as reflected in the diplomatic documents runs the danger of overlooking the real motives which impelled men to act as they did at the time. It is futile to hope to understand the mighty soaring flight of history by gathering up the feathers covering the ground. The more the powers of this earth practise the art of concealing their motives from the very start of an action leading to a crisis, and the more consciously their diplomatic technique strives to protect itself from incriminating exposure to the eyes of public opinion and posterity, the more imperative is the duty of history to penetrate the surface of external events and sound the depths of interpretation, and to throw light upon the artificially obscured motives. Only in this way can the actual historical responsibility for a great crisis be determined.

If the political will of the French in July, 1870, and its share of responsibility for the war are to be uncovered, it is necessary to trace the historical line back through the preceding seven years, as we have attempted to do on the basis of the documents. The utterances of the last critical moments must be judged by the larger substance. Furthermore the decisive days of the crisis must be looked at in the light of the source which reflects most clearly the picture of a policy which found it necessary to veil itself on all sides in a heavy shroud. We refer once more to the reports of Prince Metternich, who for seven years was in closest touch with the secret forces of the Napoleonic policy and frequently strove with all his might to identify himself with its aims. To this trusty confidant of French policies the Emperor and his henchmen gave an insight into their plans all the more because they hoped to win him over at any cost to their side. For this reason the testimony of the Austrian ambassador is more decisive evidence than the rest of the abundant official material including the recently published Prussian documents. For it is not so much the technical, diplomatic superficialities or the oft recounted external incidents which tell; it is rather their inherent dynamics and their internal relations. Even the counter-part played by Bismarck, which has been so minutely investigated, is of secondary importance in comparison with the French rôle which from the very beginning was played with breathless speed and persistent determination.

First of all it is important to establish how an observer who, like Prince Metternich, was always accustomed to see things in a French light reacted at first to the crisis caused by the Spanish succession. He was so far from believing that an alleged insult to France could be used as the motif for a great action that he expressed to the Emperor and Gramont the amicable view that in this question Bismarck could well afford to concede a diplomatic victory to the French if he could in return therefor count upon friendly cooperation in other more important questions, for example in the German question. The Emperor and his ministers reached the opposing conclusion from the very outset. They decided to magnify the question of succession into a great crisis and if possible to make it the motive for war, in order thus to be able to interfere effectively in the German question.

The declarations decided upon in the ministerial council, meeting with Napoleon in the chair, which

Gramont and Ollivier made on July 6 to the legislature (textually even more provocative than the official text published later), were planned from the start as a measure which, contrary to diplomatic usage, intended to open the discussion by breaking all bridges immediately, leaving Prussia only the choice between an unparalleled humiliation or war. Metternich later tried to justify this unbridled language as necessary to arouse French patriotism, which could only be inspired by such insults, and as a strategic measure which made open preparations for war permissible. The decisive question of course is: What was the intention of the French statesmen in inaugurating this action? Here too the reports of Metternich are a source of the highest value, for during the session of the chamber he was first in the company of the Emperor, then with the Empress, and then he spoke to Ollivier immediately after the session, and each of them at this time concealed nothing from the Austrian representative.

Metternich found the imperial couple in the same mood, Napoleon with a delighted, beaming face,[34] Eugenie so strongly in favor of war that he (who did not yet believe that they were serious) was tempted to tease her a bit.[35] She seemed to him "ten years younger at the thought of a political triumph or a war." Both were interested most in the question of the consequences of their preliminary step. As soon as the ambassador mentioned the possibility of a retreat on Prussia's part, Napoleon interrupted him excitedly with the words: "Do you really believe that Bismarck *can* turn back in the face of our stringent call to order?", emphasizing that "we must be prepared for any eventuality, it is a question of speed", and ending with the question: "Can we count on Austria?" The thoughts of the Empress were not dissimilar: "If Bismarck retreats, it will be a severe humiliation for him, from which he will never recover." She too thought only of the other solution. Even more unrestrained than the imperial couple was Ollivier, who, fresh from his oratorical triumph in the legislature, said to the ambassador: "It is no longer the Rouhers and La Valettes who shape the policies of France. It is I, a minister of the people, coming from the people, feeling with the people, I, a minister responsible to the nation, who have conducted this matter with the patriotic resolve which you know characterizes me. We have reached the unanimous decision that we must march, we have carried the chamber away, we shall carry the nation away. In two weeks we shall have 400,000 men on the Saar, and we shall wage war as in 1793. We shall arm the people and they will storm to the frontier." [36]

At the beginning of the action that was the language of the "man of peace," who had once been rated a friend of Prussia, the language of the minister who was not even initiated into the real secrets of Napoleon's policy—good evidence of the power of tradition in this France, and proof of how correct Napoleon's judgment of this pacifist had been, who became a *miles gloriosus* at the first opportunity. Even in the chamber he had spoken in hyperboles: "Whenever, as history proves, France has shown herself firm, Europe has bowed before the will of France." But in private conversation pride and temperament drove him still farther, as is always the case with those who have a new language to speak and lose all their restraint in an unaccustomed field. The historian Ollivier later tried for an entire generation to prove that he had no share at all in making the war, that Bismarck purposely raised the problem of the Spanish candidacy in order to make it the pretext for war. He knows nothing of the words which the minister Ollivier pronounced to the Austrian ambassador on the afternoon of July 6. Yet these very words which breathe but the one desire, namely to use this pretext hotheadedly as a motive for war, prove conclusively that from the first hour of the crisis on Ollivier was the man "of light heart," as he is known in history.

It was the pretext which carried Napoleon and his henchmen away. Metternich, who during these days was much more critical and sceptical than usual, told the Duke of Gramont to his face on July 8: "You simply seized the opportunity blindly, following the proverb that a good opportunity comes but once, and you thought it necessary to seize it by the horns in order to win a diplomatic victory or to wage war on a basis which would not stir the German spirit against you." "That is well said," replied Gramont with flattered vanity. "Won't you initiate your chancellor into the secret of this game of dice? Herr von Beust will be pleased with me. He must have been prepared for such a bold step on my part." [37]

That remark touched upon the decisive point which conditioned the action of Napoleon and his henchmen from the beginning. Napoleon's first question had been whether he could count on Austria. In the following days the same question was addressed to Italy. But before a very reserved reply came from Vienna, Gramont in the ministerial council had lightheartedly replied to a question of the minister of war by declaring that Austria would in case of war station an observation corps on the frontier and in this manner engage a part of the Prussian forces. "That is the least you would do, isn't it?" he asked the surprised Austrian confidently, adding: "but I hope you will not stop there." Napoleon was firm in his conviction that the moral ties of the monarchical letters of September, 1869, combined with the irresistible pressure of the situation, would make the Austro-Hungarian Monarchy his ally, in spite of all reservations. Gramont, only partly initiated into the negotiations, even assumed a positive obligation on Austria's part, though Beust had never sanctioned this. It was this notion which spurred the Emperor and his minister on, and if in the sequel they were sometimes more hesitant and doubtful, the reason for this was primarily that they hoped thus to make participation easier for their ally.

Was it still necessary, as Ollivier vaunted, "to carry the nation away"? On July 5, the day before the session of the chamber, Granier de Cassagnac in his "Pays" had published an article entitled "Le Rhin français," which noisily presented to the Emperor those claims which had long been the secret of his policy. "The possession of the left bank of the Rhine," he wrote, "is for France not a matter of pride, which would be reprehensible, nor is it a challenge to the German nation, which would be ridiculous; it is a concern for security, which is defensible and legitimate. We have no longer any protecting buffer states or confederation between Prussia and ourselves. In place of this vanished security we need another. The first cannon shot will restore it to us."

That was the long sought goal of the Emperor, for the sake of which he had helped to bring about the war of 1866 and pursued his unhappy policy of compensations thereafter. The striving for an alliance which began in the spring of 1867 had the object of snatching the prize in the eleventh hour. And now at the outset of the crisis the cry arose and soon found an echo in every camp, becoming so strong through the proclamation of July 6 that nothing remained for the Emperor but submission. The instincts which he had always flattered for the sake of his throne demanded satisfaction, and the nation, which the leaders planned to carry away, itself carried away the leaders so irresistibly that, once they had taken the first step, there was no stopping without abandoning their leadership.

It was natural that the first step involved a second and that the hidden causes of the crisis soon threatened to break through the mere external pretext. On July 13 the Austrian military attaché said: "For six days now the French statesmen have left the ground of the Hohenzollern candidacy and have taken their stand exclusively by the general necessity of precipitating war with Prussia and finally fighting it through. After a few days it seemed probable that the warnings of the great powers in Berlin would meet with success and that by the withdrawal of the Hohenzollern candidate the *casus belli* would disappear without particular humiliation for Prussia. Was France to acquiesce in such an outcome, after her lively preparations, or was she to use the occasion for securing guarantees for the future and bringing up the German question again, even at the risk of war? A policy which admittedly aimed at the humiliation of Prussia or war and had so little fear of the second alternative, was almost obliged to follow up the first successful offensive with a second as soon as the formal object had been attained. And so Emile de Girrardin published an article in the "Liberté" of July 9, formulating the alternative of a congress or a war, but a congress on condition that the German fortresses (Mainz, Cologne and Landau) be dismantled. And if the Prussians refused, they were to be beaten back across the Rhine and forced to evacuate the left bank. On the very next day the official "Moniteur" in an editorial authorized by the ministry took up this strain. As a minimum satisfaction, to which France was entitled, and as a minimum demand, which France must make, it listed the exact observance of the letter and spirit of the Peace of Prague, including the freedom of the southern states (i. e. abandonment of their alliances with the north), the evacuation of Mainz, Prussia's renunciation of all influence south of the Main, and the settlement of the North Schleswig question. If these claims were not satisfied, the article said, the French demands would be increased. Through the flimsy veil of Spanish dynastic questions we see lurking those same problems which French politics had for the past few years tried to use as the basis for a program of joint action with Austria. The Salzburg memorandum is only one of many examples. On the very next day the newspaper demands were reechoed in the chamber, which, mindful of its new parliamentary rights, now assumed an aggressive rôle.

In the session of the corps législatif of July 11 the extreme Left asked the ministers whether they intended to introduce "other questions" into the conflict with Prussia. The Right prevented Gramont in a turbulent debate from replying to the question in the negative. Ollivier was inclined to yield to this pressure, for Metternich reported shortly before 6 P. M. of July 11 that "Gramont is somewhat at odds with Ollivier, who would like to link 'other questions' with the Hohenzollern question in order to make war inevitable, while Gramont wishes peace in case the King of Prussia yields." [38] The historian Ollivier is once again so concerned with proving his peaceful intentions that he forgets that the statesman Ollivier took an even more warlike stand in this question than the irascible foreign minister. We have a letter of Ollivier to Napoleon, written at 6 P. M., wherein he describes the events of the legislative session. He reported that the Right was loudly declaring that there must be no halt, that other questions should be raised, that the Peace of Prague should be discussed and that Prussia must be resolutely confronted with the alternative of a congress (with the program of the German question) or war. The Left too, he writes, is raising the same cry (Gambetta had already made the demand for the dismantling of the German forts his own!) and both sides threaten to attack the cabinet if it stops after the settlement of the Spanish succession, while Thiers advises against it. It was under the influence of this report that late in the evening of July 11, not long before midnight, Napoleon asked Prince Metternich: "Do you not think that it is necessary to complicate the question?" The ambassador, true to the policy pursued by Beust for the past three years, urgently advised against it and was instrumental in the abandonment of the plan. But he added to his report to Vienna the important sentence: "Emperor Napoleon will try a new expedient. Tomorrow, Tuesday, he will order the mobilization of the first grade, without modifying the status of the question, and he believes that this step will make war inevitable." [39] Apparently the only concern of Napoleon and his advisers at this time was to make sure of war and not get off the track. The Austrians at least had the impression that the only question was how the war could be most effectively staged. The Austrian military attaché too stated at the end of a telegram sent to Vienna during the night of July 11–12: "I estimate that France has an advantage of eight or ten days so far as time is concernd. War is here demanded on every side, the excitement is very great, the occasion popular, the decision dangerous; certainly the Empire would never again have such opportunities and advantages in point of time. Count Bismarck has now only the choice between war and a second Olmütz." On July 12 at noon the news of the renunciation of Prince Leopold reached Paris. Ollivier apparently much relieved, took it to the chamber himself. "And the Peace of Prague—what of that?" was the retort. The deputy Clément Duvernois introduced an interpellation asking what guarantees the cabinet had secured or expected to secure to avoid a recurrence of trouble with Prussia. A stormy outburst showed the majority to be in favor of war. The hour had come when the spirits which had been summoned had won the upper hand. To be sure Austria had advised against seeking a guarantee in the shape of a complication of the dispute through German questions. A despatch from Beust written at noon, July 12 (which arrived in Paris that afternoon and must have been communicated by Metternich) clearly expressed the opinion of the ambassador. Hence this course had to be abandoned and another found.

Gramont had already found it. At this very time (3 P. M. of July 12) he suggested to the ambassador of the North German Confederation that King William by a letter to Napoleon which was to be published should settle the matter once and for all and thus "contribute toward the appeasement of public opinion." Meanwhile Napoleon, upon hearing of the withdrawal of the Hohenzollern prince, had expressed sentiments of peace. But even the excited, martial greeting of the populace on his trip from St. Cloud to the Tuileries made a deep impression upon him. In St. Cloud he found feverish excitement. The Empire is lost! was the cry on all sides. What a disgrace! cried the Empress to her consort. And General Bourbaki, in true theatrical fashion, threw his sword upon the table because he no longer wished to wear it. The news of the Duvernois interpellation was the last straw for the unnerved Emperor. When at this moment Gramont appeared with his proposal, Napoleon sanctioned the message to Benedetti (7 P. M.) containing the well-known demand upon King William.

The meaning of all this becomes clear from the prelude of the last few days. The Olmütz which was to be prepared for the Prussians was simply transferred to another field. If the German question were dragged in, it was to be feared that the Germans would be unanimous in defence, in case of war. That was why Vienna advised against this course. And so the original line of action was resumed, and an Olmütz in the field of dynastic questions, as it were, was prepared. Only diplomatic caution, as well as consideration for Austria and the South Germans, as paradoxical as this seems, had brought about such a formal restriction of the demand for guarantees, which with its demand for a royal letter of apology, brought war a step closer, to be sure. The historian Ollivier would fain attribute the *peripetia* to the influence of Gramont brought to bear upon the Emperor late in the afternoon of July 12, but does it not appear from the reports of Metternich that on July 11 both Ollivier and the Emperor considered measures designed to make war inevitable? If on the next day they were more peaceably inclined, this does not prove that they were willing to oppose a clamor for war which they themselves had originated. The passions which beset them forced them to continue the course begun on July 5.

Nevertheless Napoleon and Gramont did not plan to precipitate war by their demand for the letter of apology. Rather was it their intention to protract the negotiations in this way in order to give them an even greater advantage with respect to preparedness —a consideration which since Napoleon's hint of July 6 played a decisive part. Those who recall the negotiations between Archduke Albrecht and General Lebrun will not doubt the importance of this motive for the encouragement and military cooperation of the Austrians. At every opportunity Prince Metternich was informed of the extent of this advantage.

This is the kernel of the problem concerning the origins of the war, studied with the same intensity by historians and politicians, and a document which has come to light only recently serves to illuminate brilliantly these secret motives of the French statesmen. Let us listen to the crown witness, whose confession lifts the veil. The Duc de Gramont declared on the afternoon of July 18 to the Danish minister Count Moltke-Hvitfeldt and to the Danish general Raaslöff, whom he sought to drag into the war on the side of the Triple Alliance by offering them Schleswig: "We have an advantage of ten or eleven days over the Prussians with respect to military preparations. We should have had even more if we could have protracted the negotiations still more, as we had wished. Unfortunately the King of Prussia has insulted us, and this fact made it necessary to break off negotiations at once." [40]

Gramont was thinking here of the Ems despatch. It is well known that in Ems itself no insult was offered. In fact Gramont admitted this on the previous day to the Bavarian minister. The historical import of the Ems despatch then lies not in the fact that it broke off peaceful negotiations by an offensive act which rendered war inevitable, but rather, as the French foreign minister admitted, in the fact that it disturbed the war-plotting intrigue of the French and their plan of protracting the negotiations for the sake of winning time for further preparations. If this is granted, the despatch must be interpreted as a defensive act on Bismarck's part which with unerring instinct tore the veil from the ambiguities designed to secure for the bellicose French the most favorable moment for action. Was it Bismarck's duty to wait patiently for the moment which suited his opponent best? After the challenges of the past week there could be no doubt what the French wanted, and as for Bismarck's revision of the despatch, it must be judged in the light of the language which the official French governmental organs had been using. If the despatch has been compared with the blare of a trumpet, it was but a fitting answer to the warlike spirit which had long robbed the French statesmen of their senses. For the question of guilt therefore the Ems despatch—the fact that it is hardly mentioned in the Austrian diplomatic correspondence can scarcely be due to chance—must be regarded as of secondary importance, and the French conception, which seizes upon the despatch as the decisive factor—the memoirs of Lord Grey show how the legend continues to live—seeks to make an artificially isolated diplomatic event of a fragmentary nature the key to the catastrophe, instead of looking at it in its larger aspect. The bomb merely exploded too soon, or rather the French felt constrained to light the fuse a little earlier than they had planned.

The possibility of a congress, cropping up on July 14–15, is also a mere episode in the diplomatic negotiations. To be sure, Napoleon on the evening of July 14 wanted to propose a congress to settle all disputed points, and on the following day proposed the cooperation of Austria and Italy for this purpose. But the plan of a congress, which really aimed at intervention rather than peace, was only a means of forcing the other two powers to follow him and meanwhile to improve upon the handicap which he already enjoyed. Napoleon's real designs appear from his fatalistic utterances to Count Vitzthum on the morning of July 15. He warned the Austrians to station an observation corps in Bohemia and added significantly: "The congress must not prevent us from making war." But even this little side-show, so characteristic of the half-hearted Emperor, aroused Gramont's mistrust, so that on the evening of July 15 he exclaimed to Count Vitzthum in sheer excitement that he would throw down his portfolio if the Emperor mentioned it again. "The idea of speaking of a congress at this time! We have called our reserves, and Marshal Leboeuf declared only yesterday that we are prepared from tip to toe." But after this scene Metternich said to Vitzthum: "I am glad you saw him, for now you can support me in assuring Vienna that it would be hopeless to try to talk sense to a man who has manifestly lost his head and is *non compos.*" The passion for war was already more powerful than any deliberate war plans, which welcomed every possible chance for diplomatic gains before actually unleashing war.

The reaction of the events of these weeks upon the representative of that power which the French thought was morally beholden to them, is all the more important because Metternich had not become an opponent of French policy; on the contrary he was passionately in favor of joining France once the issue of war had been clearly joined, all this in spite of his severe criticism of her methods. Beust too had been outspoken in his condemnation of these methods and had repeatedly urged conciliation as late even as July 13. Although the will for war on the part of France was stronger than his longing for revenge, which was hedged in by all sorts of reservations, yet he was personally inclined to take the initial military steps which Napoleon expected of Austrian polity.

At any rate, after war had been determined upon, Gramont believed he could carry away the Austrians with the same enthusiasm which marked his own plunge into the disastrous adventure. On July 17, while a French general was on his way to Berlin with the declaration of war, he wrote to Beust: "If I could have chosen the hour for action, I should, of course, have made sure to perfect our treaties and to bring about an agreement to suit our convenience, an agreement which I must now ask you to reach in all haste." He asked for permission to have 70,000 or 80,000 Italians march through Tyrol to Bavaria; he requested that 150,000 Austrians be stationed in Bohemia and that in addition 200,000 or 300,000 be mustered to dictate peace in Berlin. In view of this prospect, which had played the decisive rôle in all his decisions, it is no wonder that the minister exclaimed: "Never will we have such an opportunity again, never will we find such effective support, never will France be as strong as now, as well armed and equipped and so full of enthusiasm. . . . At the moment I write this I feel that the spirit which animates me is the spirit of all France, the spirit of the Emperor and the army. . . . In a few hours you can have the preliminaries on paper, which will suffice to bind us and which we will perfect while the troops are advancing." [41]

The considerations of domestic and foreign policy which, in the Austrian council of war of July 18, were opposed to Austria's declaration of war are well known. They were primarily the opposition of Andrassy and the menacing pressure of Russia. Since no binding tie existed, the impetuous urging of Archduke Albrecht and of Kuhn, the minister of war, proved just as unsuccessful as the somewhat more diplomatic recommendation of the chancellor. The attempts of Paris to continue to spin the threads of an Austro-Italian mediation (on the basis of a *status quo*, including the annulment of the South

German treaties of alliance) are of minor importance for the question of war or peace and serve only the purpose of setting in motion the machinery established by the Triple Alliance in 1869, the hope now being that the intended mediation would develop into cooperation. The subsequent attempts to effect a Triple Alliance upon a new contractual basis was definitely frustrated only by the battle of Wörth.

Of course the measure of Napoleon's personal responsibility during the last days, which were marked by some hesitation and evasion on his part, can not be determined as clearly as it could in 1863–1866, when he was the sovereign master of the fate of nations. But it does not affect his deeper historical responsibility for a war of which he himself said to a friend on March 2, 1871: "I admit that we were the aggressors." [1]

It is, however, very important for the judgment of history to determine with what political aims Napoleon and his henchmen went into the war. A state's will to war at the hour of the outbreak of hostilities must be judged in part at least by the positive objectives which that state has set itself or has officially communicated to a third party. After we have

---

[1] Letters of Emperor Napoleon III to Countess Louise de Mercy-Argenteau. Velhagen und Klasings Monatshefte, September, 1906.

endeavored to uncover this motive, so far as the documents reveal it, thus touching upon a problem which has hitherto been too much neglected by other investigators, we will have completed our delineation of Napoleon's policy.

XI

WITH soldierly frankness the French military attaché in Berlin, Colonel Stoffel, discussed the true cause of the war at the time of its outbreak. He said that the war was the result of the preponderance of Prussia since 1866 and that this preponderance required France to secure her boundaries. Such security, he felt, she could attain only by acquiring the German territory west of the Rhine, and French possession of the Rhine alone could guarantee the peace between the two nations. These utterances are in agreement with the facts as we have revealed them according to the documents, except that the documents go even farther and show that already prior to the war of 1866 Napoleon had a Rhine policy and by an unsuccessful intrigue had himself helped to establish the order which later he believed he could subvert only by conquering the Rhine. This is corroborated by the fact that as late as August 6, the day of the battle of Wörth,

Prince Metternich, who had a deeper insight than anyone else into the Napoleonic policies of 1863-1870, spoke outright of the Rhine as the chief war aim. This fact, usually kept dark in France nowadays, was emphasized on September 18, 1919, by the French socialist J. Longuet in a parliamentary address, when he said that it should not be forgotten that the yearning for the left bank of the Rhine was responsible for the war of 1870.

In July, 1870, to be sure, French diplomacy had to speak a quite different language abroad. The louder the rabble in Paris clamored for the Rhine, the more zealously did France try to make the outside world believe that she was waging no war of aggression. Although there was little enough serious hope of winning over the South German states, the French government, in all declarations made prior to the final decision of South Germany, made a particular point of stating that it did not intend to take an inch of German soil and wished merely to check the further growth of Prussia. Gramont even went so far as expressly to disavow to the Bavarian minister the demands for the Rhine voiced by the Paris press and was careful to have this noble renunciation loudly proclaimed especially in the Viennese press, so that public sentiment in German Austria might not be estranged but might be prepared for a war on the side of France.

But did these formal declarations, which culminated in Napoleon's war manifesto of July 23, contain the whole truth, or did they admit of evasion and doubtful interpretation? It has already been mentioned that Denmark was to receive as the minimum price of her cooperation all of Schleswig—in other words territory of distinctly German stamp which had been hotly contested for a generation. And what the French were prepared to offer Austria in the event of cooperation, is clear from the negotiations carried on ever since 1866. There can be no doubt that in case of victory not only Silesia would have changed hands; it is more than likely that the old Austrian craving for Bavarian territory would have cropped up again too. And what of the specifically French war objectives?

While publicly stressing non-annexation, Paris found it necessary to resort once more to the substitute for pure annexation which it had for years advocated as a solution compatible with German self-respect and national consciousness, and sugared with so many secret hopes. The autonomous Rhineland state appears once more as a French war aim in the decisive hour. At any rate the French minister in Stuttgart allowed this rather obscure remark to escape him: according to the plans made in Paris in the last few years it is the French aim, in case of victory, to establish a state of about five million inhabitants along the Rhine, perhaps for the King of Hannover." Gramont too spoke to the Bavarian minister of a restoration and enlargement of Hannover in order to destroy the Prussian preponderance. Although he considered it more expedient not to mention the Rhineland state expressly, he revealed his intention in another way by hinting at the "annulment" of Baden as a Prussian subsidiary. It will be remembered that it was Gramont too who as early as April, 1867, had offered the Austrians South Germany as far as the Black Forest and had shown a special French interest only for Baden. These few points will suffice to disclose the extent of French "renunciation" with respect to German soil. In reverting to the old idea of a neutral state along the Rhine, as a policy which ought to prove acceptable to Europe, France realized of course that in case the treaty of peace were really dictated in Berlin, this modest policy, which was always considered a minimum requirement, would not have to stand.

But the French revealed not only individual phases of their war program. At one point they developed the program in its entirety, though in a discreet form. We refer to the declaration which Gramont early in August was indiscreet enough to make to the Russian chargé in official form, describing it expressly as containing the minimum demands of France.[42] This list includes annexation pure and simple. In demanding the cession of the Saar basin Gramont clearly violated the solemn promise not to claim even a bit of German territory. As for the boundaries of 1814, which ever since 1860 were regarded as the most modest satisfaction of French needs, French diplomacy was accustomed to regard them as resting on an old legal title. But the sum total of the German territorial modifications, which France communicated without hesitation to this friend of Prussia, is even more impressive. It included the reduction of Prussia to the boundaries of 1866 and restoration of the dispossessed; enlargement of the middle states at the expense of ancient Prussian territory, and "constitution of state groups in Germany which would permanently break the Prussian supremacy." This formula expresses the well-known aim of dividing Germany into as many equally large states as possible, the aim which had been made the basis of the Franco-Austrian negotiations of 1869. No evidence is necessary to prove that in this grouping the neutralized Rhineland state with a generous allotment of territory was to play an important part and would in a sense have symbolized the federalistic dismemberment of Germany.

In one respect the war aims communicated by Gramont to the Russians contain a surprise—a feature which at the same time explains the reason why they were communicated at all. At the end the French minister asked the Russian government the official question what it planned to do if the French army should reach Berlin and offer Danzig to Russia in return for her neutrality. This free disposition of German territory, which thus revealed designs even against the eastern German frontier, is the last official expression of the French war aims, made only a short time before the first skirmish at Weissenburg.

In the light of all these French plans, which, be it noted, must be regarded as minimum demands, it becomes clear how perfidious was the war manifesto wherein Napoleon announced to the world his desire that "the peoples forming the great Germanic nation shall be free to control their own destinies." The announcement of the manifesto that it was planned to establish an order "guaranteeing our security for the future" is of the same ilk. The persistent use of such phrases for centuries did not serve to make them more plausible. The picture of the Germany of the Peace of Westphalia, exposed on every side to invasion and disruption, and with all internal bonds loosened to a degree of utter defenselessness—this was the historical ideal of the past which dominated the plans of the present. It was "the great idea" of the French policy, according to Thiers, to disorganize the German state to such an extent that security and aggrandizement would fall to the happy lot of its French neighbor.

Against this menace, which had barely been avoided in 1866, the Germans had to defend their unity and independence in 1870. In this latter year it was the last echo of those Napoleonic speculations which we discovered as being the secret forces impelling the empire for the seven years between 1863 and 1870. But during a more recent period of seven years, from 1919 to 1926, we have learned by experience that the rhythm of French history is still guided by its initial principle, that this nation, impelled by the force of tradition, can not resist the evil temptations which surround it.

The policy of Napoleon and the French, which opposed Germany's national right of self-determination, led to the war of 1870. Was it justifiable for this policy to defend its fateful course of action before the bars of history by pleading the "security" of France? Is such justification admissible? We have seen how after 1866 the motive of security gradually met the requirements of the new situation and supplanted that of aggrandizement. But it was only a new name for an old concept—the concept of national frontiers, Romano-Gallic reminiscences, pseudo-historical feudal rights and other attempts to clothe gross reality in a palliating mantle of ideas. Two generations earlier the attainment of the national frontiers had been looked upon in France as a sacred tradition. "It is the doctrine of the scholar," said Sorel, "the creed of the poet, the ambition of the popular leader, of the kings the ministers the generals the political meetings and the committees; it is a question of interests for the economist, a reason of state for the politician, a national dream." All these spheres of life forthwith seized upon the motive of security, and thus revived once more a great historical tradition. This tradition, though it spoke in terms of defence, had in reality an offensive purpose, for it strove to disturb or diminish the national unity of its neighbor. It was animated by the theory that its own security, unity and peace could be maintained only if that neighbor were doomed to insecurity, disunity and unrest, and in advocating this theory it violated the unwritten law of morality which guides the life of nations and sets bounds to the egoism of national interests.

The struggles of the past are of interest for the

historical consciousness of the European nations only when their motives and impulses live on in the present as a determining factor. The line which runs from Louis XIV directly to Napoleon III becomes in the end a prime cause for the war of 1870–1871. This fact was clear to the generation which fought that war. To the numerous judgments of other nations we may add the opinion of the American minister Bancroft, the renowned historian. On October 12, 1870, he spoke the following confidential words in the Berlin foreign office: "The leading statesmen as well as public opinion in America regard the present war essentially as an act of self-defence on Germany's part, and the outstanding task is to insure Germany permanently, by a better system of frontiers, against new wars of aggression on the part of her western neighbors, of which the past three centuries have brought so large a number." [1]

The real facts began to be obscured when, with the formation of the great coalition against Germany, the French conception was adopted by the political allies of France. And since the World War the question of the causes of the war of 1870 was, for political reasons, still more obscured and sup-

[1] Undersecretary von Thile to the minister in Washington, Baron von Gerolt. Strictly confidential, October 13, 1870 (Berlin Foreign Office).

planted by a legend which described the latter as merely a step preliminary to the former. The causes of both wars were merged in one large question of guilt, so presented that those who, in France or in countries intellectually dependent upon her, believed in the exclusive or principal responsibility of Germany for the World War, were led to believe also the legend that France was attacked by Germany in 1870. But while the French undertook to reconstruct a fictitious past and to invent the story of the French lamb and the German wolf, it happened that the newly aroused spirit of their historical Rhineland policy, endowed with a new halo and unhampered by diplomatic considerations, has in recent years since the World War given ever more damaging testimony of them. What we have detected as the secret motive power of French politics ever since 1815 and as the Napoleonic ambition which from 1863 on led to the catastrophe, now became more irresistible than ever before. Almost all parties, with a few exceptions, now endorsed the claim for the Rhine, and all along the line scholarship, animated by a spirit which Albert Sorel had once castigated, argued the historical right of that claim, enlisting self-interest and sentiment in the service of a consistent endeavor, which varied but in the details of method and advocated now annexation pure and simple and now some form of Rhineland state, either neutral or at least independent of Prussia and in any case exposed to penetration. This device, of course, had always been the first step toward conquest, and during the dark days of confusion after 1919 it found, even in Germany, sympathetic fools and treacherous advocates who did not realize whose interests would be served by any change in the established order along the Rhine.

If the causes of the war of 1870 are to be linked and associated with those of the World War, well and good. History justifies such a procedure, but not in the sense in which the enemies of Germany, who would make her alone responsible for the World War, interpret it. The French national tradition which drove Napoleon III into the war and brought about the fateful clash between the historical Rhineland policy of the French and the right of self-determination of the German people is the cradle of that spirit of revenge which played so important a part in bringing about the international tension leading to the World War. The same spirit which inspired the secret forces of the French national soul has imposed upon it a large measure of guilt before the bars of mankind. Inasmuch as this spirit prevents a permanent reconciliation of the two nations after the catastrophe, it has remained to this day the most serious obstruction to all hopes for future pacific intercourse among the nations of Europe.

END

NOTES

The above presentation, from 1863 on, is based altogether upon the documents contained in Hermann Oncken's *Die Rheinpolitik Kaiser Napoleons III von 1863 bis 1870 und der Ursprung des Krieges von 1870–1871. Nach den Staatsakten von Österreich, Preussen und den süddeutschen Mittelstaaten* (3 volumes, Deutsche Verlagsanstalt, Stuttgart, Berlin and Leipzig, 1926). The following notes present the original text of but a few of the most interesting passages selected from these documents. Lack of space makes it impossible to give more than a brief selection here. It is hoped, however, that the following pages will prove an incentive for students of history to consult Professor Oncken's original work.

For a general introduction to the subject the reader is referred to another work by Professor Oncken, *Die historische Rheinpolitik der Franzosen* (Stuttgart and Gotha, 1922), which has appeared in English as *The Historical Rhine Policy of the French* (New York, B. W. Huebsch, 1923).

[1] Prince Metternich to Count Rechberg, March 5, 1863. "Ainsi, j'ai dit, une fois que les impatiences de l'Impéra-

trice me mettaient hors de moi: ce que Vous voulez avant tout, c'est pouvoir faire une proclamation aux Français dans laquelle Vous annonceriez que ce que Vos armes n'ont pas pu amener, Votre habileté l'a obtenu. L'Italie libre jusqu'à l'Adriatique . . . , la Pologne reconstituée aux dépens des traités de 1815, le Rhin devenue fleuve français—voilà ce que Vous voulez." (Oncken, *Die Rheinpolitik Napoleons III,* vol. I, p. 12.)

[2] Count Goltz to King William I, February 9, 1864.

"Als ich ihm [Drouyn de Lhuys] bemerkbar machte, dass wir keine solche Kompensationen zu bieten hätten, äusserte er, für Frankreich würde eine geringe Rektifikation der Grenze genügen, da gebe es z. B. Landau, welches, soviel er wisse, 1814 Frankreich hätte verbleiben sollen. Er erörterte demnächst die Idee, aus der preussischen Rheinprovinz einen unabhängigen, neutralen Staat nach dem Muster Belgiens zu bilden—ein Gedanke, welcher bereits öfters vom Kaiser Napoleon geäussert worden ist. Meine Frage, ob denn dieser Staat zum Deutschen Bunde gehören sollte, beantwortete er verneinend." (Ibid., vol. I, p. 29.)

[3] Count Solms to Bismarck, May 30, 1869.

[Words of Minister André, chief of cabinet under Drouyn de Lhuys.]

"Wenn man hier die Politik recht verstanden hätte, müssten wir jetzt den Rhein haben. Unser Traktat mit Österreich sicherte uns, wenn es siegte, den Rhein. Sie wissen dies längst, deshalb brauche ich kein Geheimnis daraus zu machen. Allerdings war der Rhein in dem Vertrage ausdrücklich genannt, aber unter den "compensations" war eben nur das linke Rheinufer verstanden. Drouyn de Lhuys wollte nun einfach genau denselben Vertrag mit Preussen schliessen." (Ibid., vol. I, p. 290.)

[4] Memoirs of the Duke of Persigny, p. 332 ff.

"Or du moment que, au lieu d'une grande puissance comme la Prusse, nous n'aurions plus sur notre frontière découverte que des états allemands placés entre nous comme des tampons, pour amortir les chocs, il ne resterait plus rien de l'œuvre de 1815; nous ne serions plus menacés d'aucun côté . . . Il suffirait de reveiller les souvenirs des premiers temps de notre histoire, de créer une confédération des Gaules, formée de la Hollande, de la Belgique, du Luxembourg, des États du Rhin et de la France, pour reconquérir nos frontières naturelles." (Ibid., vol. I, p. 212 f.)

[5] Prince Metternich to Count Mensdorff, April 29, 1866.

"Mr. Drouyn de Lhuys m'a dit: Der Kaiser würde im Falle, dass das Resultat des Krieges eine Offensivverstärkung Deutschlands unter preussischer oder österreichischer Oberleitung zur Folge hätte, gewisse Kompensationen oder Garantien verlangen. Er glaubt, dass, wenn wir aber eine Neutralisierung der Rheinlande sous une dynastie neutrale quoique allemande versprechen könnten, de manière qu'il serait également interdit à la France et à l'Allemagne d'y toucher, so würde Frankreich uns und unsre Freunde in Deutschland gerne vergrössern." (Ibid., vol. I, p. 144.)

[6] French draft of an alliance drawn up by the secret mission of Prince Napoleon and General Kiss (May 30, 1866).

"7. La paix se fera sous les conditions suivantes . . . Pour la France le territoire entre Moselle et Rhin sans Coblence ni Mayence, 1,855,000 âmes savoir: 500,000 Prusse, 1,100,000 Bavière, Birkenfeld 35,000, Homburg 27,000, Darmstadt 21,300." (Ibid., vol. I, p. 244.)

[7] Prince Metternich to Count Mensdorff, June 6, 1866.

"L'Empereur . . . me fit les confidences suivantes qui méritent d'être signalées: . . . J'ai surtout laissé s'avançer la Prusse, me disant que le moment venu de s'assurer de moi, on me ferait un pont d'or. Les provinces du Rhin en perspective lointaine m'ont longtemps fait hésiter à faire mon choix." (Ibid., vol. I, p. 253.)

[8] Duke of Gramont to Drouyn de Lhuys, June 12, 1866.

"Le Gouvernement autrichien n'aurait aucune objection à élever contre un remaniement territorial qui, en agrandissant la Saxe, le Wurtemberg, et même la Bavière, aux dépens de princes mediatisés, ferait des provinces rhenanes un nouvel État allemand, indépendant." (Origines diplomatiques, 10, p. 142–147; Oncken, op. cit., vol. I, p. 268.)

[9] For further details concerning the plan of conquest along the Rhine, of July 5, 1866, see Oncken, op cit., vol. I, p. 303.

[10] Count Benedetti to Bismarck, August 5, 1866.

"Je reçois de Vichy le projet de convention secrète que vous trouverez ci-joint en copie. . . . Projet de convention. Article 1er. L'Empire français rentre en possession des portions de territoire qui, appartenant aujourd'hui à la Prusse, avaient été comprises dans la délimitation de la France en 1814. Article 2. La Prusse s'engage à obtenir du rois de Bavière et du grand-duc de Hesse, sauf à fournir à ces princes des dédommagements, la cession des portions de territoire qu'ils possèdent sur la rive gauche du Rhin et à en transférer la possession à la France." (Ibid., vol. II, p. 22.)

[11] Count Goltz to Bismarck, August 9, 1866.

"Er [Drouyn de Lhuys] schilderte mir zugleich in lebhaften Farben die Stimmung des Landes, wie sie sich aus Berichten gewichtiger Autoritäten ergäbe, und die Gefahren für den Thron und die Dynastie, wenn Frankreich nicht eine nicht bloss illusorische, sondern reelle, wenngleich bescheiden bemessene Kompensation erhielte. Er habe, so sagte er, zwei Dynastien fallen sehen und kenne daher genau die Symptome, welche einer solchen Umwälzung vorherzugehen pflegten. Er habe sich nie darin getäuscht. Hiernach könne er mir aber versichern, dass der Thron des Kaisers Gefahr liefe, wenn Seine Majestät sich eine so immense Veränderung des Gleichgewichts ruhig gefallen liesse." (Ibid., vol. II, p. 41.)

[12] Memorial of Drouyn de Lhyus on the establishment of a Rhenish buffer state, August 8, 1866.

"Le meilleur moyen d'assurer ce résultat ne consisterait-il pas dans l'interposition d'un État neutre qui, comprenant les pays allemands situés sur la rive gauche du Rhin, supprimerait à la fois tout contact et toute cause de rivalité entre la France et la Prusse." (Ibid., vol. II, p. 38.)

[13] Empress Eugenie to Prince Metternich, August 13, 1866.

"Est-ce Vous dire de perdre courage, bien au contraire, le moment viendra et alors qui sait . . . en attendant je crois qu'il est de votre intérêt comme du nôtre de ne pas jeter de la méfiance en Prusse et de ne pas hâter ou faire naître des circonstances qui pourraient être mauvaises pour tous à présent. La France si elle touche une fois à l'idée du Rhin, suivra, croyez-moi, cette idée, aussi surement que Vous *une autre* . . . (Ibid., vol. II, p. 65.)

[14] French memorial on a Franco-Prussian secret treaty at the expense of Belgium. No date (about August 15, 1866).

"Si la France se place hardiment sur le terrain des nationalités, il importe d'établir, des à present, qu'il n'existe pas une nationalité belge, et de fixer ce point essentiel avec la Prusse." (Ibid., vol. II, p. 81.)

[15] Rouher to Count Benedetti, August 16, 1866.

"En premier lieu, réunissant dans une même pensée les questions des frontières de 1814 et de l'annexion de la Belgique, vous devez reclamer, par un traité public, la concession de Landau, Saarlouis et du duché de Luxembourg, et la faculté, par un traité d'alliance, offensive et defensive, qui serait secret, de nous annexer ultérieurement la Belgique." (Ibid., vol. II, p. 83.)

[16] French draft of an offensive and defensive alliance between France and Prussia. About August 23, 1866.

"Art. IV. De son côté, Sa Majesté le Roi de Prusse, dans le cas où Sa Majesté l'Empereur des Français serait amené par les circonstances à faire entrer ses troupes en Belgique ou à la conquérir, accordera le concours de ses armées à la France, et la soutiendra, avec toutes ses forces de terre et de mer, envers et contre toute puissance qui, dans cette éventualité, lui déclarerait la guerre." (Ibid., vol. II, p. 95.)

[17] Count Goltz to King William I, September 11, 1866.

Marginal comment of King William I.

"Es ist also immer dieselbe Tendenz: Preussen soll Napoleon sozusagen *retten* und deshalb einen geheimen Vertrag schliessen, um gegen ein unschuldiges befreundetes Land im voraus zu konspirieren . . . Jetzt soll Preussen noch weiter gehen und einen Freund (Belgien) dem Untergang widmen!, wieder um Napoleon zu retten, und das alles, weil nur dadurch Preussen ungehindert seine Aufgabe in Deutschland erreichen könne . . . Wenn Deutschland je erführe, das ich eine französische Allianz zur Vernichtung Belgiens geschlossen habe, um dadurch Herr in Deutschland zu werden, so würden die deutschen Sympathien für Preussen sehr schwinden." (Ibid., vol. II, p. 108 f.)

[18] Prince Metternich to Baron Beust, March 7, 1867.

"Meine kleine Reise nach dem südlichen Frankreich hat mir den Beweis neuerdings geliefert, dass man im ganzen Lande nur ein Gefühl hegt, und das ist der *Preussenhass*. Überall fühlt man tief die begangenen Fehler, die auf ewig verloren gegangene Gelegenheit und hegt man die Sehnsucht nach einer 'revanche éclatante.'" (Ibid., vol. II, p. 230.)

[19] Baron Beust to Prince Metternich, April 27, 1867.

"Quelqu'en soit le résultat, poursuivit Mr. de Gramont, mon Gouvernement est prêt à toutes les éventualités; la France ne sera pas prise au dépourvu et elle ne craint pas la guerre, car tous nos armements sont achevés et nous sommes parfaitement en état d'entrer en campagne d'un instant à l'autre. Nous n'avons donc besoin de personne . . . et pourtant je viens vous proposer une alliance offensive et défensive. . . . L'Autriche et la France s'engageraient l'une vis-à-vis de l'autre à ne point déposer les armes avant d'avoir atteint certains résultats. Pour l'Empereur Napoleon, c'est la rive gauche du Rhin qu'il voudrait acquérir, c'est à dire le Palatinat bavarois et les provinces prussiennes situées sur cette rive du fleuve. Quant à la Belgique, elle resterait hors de cause et ne serait pas entamée. Pous l'Autriche, on ne laisserait arranger à sa guise toute l'Allemagne du Sud, elle pourrait en faire une Confédération à la tête de laquelle elle se placerait; elle serait même libre d'y opérer les annexions qui lui conviendraient. La France ne ferait de reserves que pour le Grand Duché de Bade, au sort duquel elle s'intéresse. La Silésie pourrait également être réunie à l'Autriche." (Ibid., vol. II, p. 361 f.)

[20] French draft of a Franco-Austrian offensive treaty (drawn up by the Duke of Gramont?), August, 1867. (Ibid., vol. II, p. 454 ff.)

[21] Prince Metternich to Baron Beust, January 25, 1868.

"Während der Kaiser in Compiegne mit dem Kriegsminister beriet, war ich Zeuge der überschwenglichen Hoffnungen, denen sich seine ergebensten Freunde hingeben. Fleury und Ney sagten mir offen, dass der Kaiser seine Massnahmen sowohl gegen innere als gegen äussere Feinde, *hinter dem Rücken* seiner Friedensminister und so sehr im geheimen treffe, dass Frankreich sowie Europa erstaunt sein würden, wie sehr der Kaiser in kürzester Zeit *zu allem bereit* stehe." (Ibid., vol. II, p. 511 f.)

[22] Lord Lyons to Lord Stanley, March 31, 1868.

. . ."some close observers who have long studied the character of the Emperor L. N. see (or fancy they see) symptoms which indicate that the idea of *a sudden declaration of war against Prussia* is present to his mind. They do *not suppose* that L. N. has yet come to any *positive decision,* but they think that, *without confiding his plans* to any one, he is *quietly* so disposing matters as to be ready if he should deem it expedient, to take *Prussia by surprise,* and produce a startling effect upon public in France." (Ibid., vol. II, p. 544.)

[23] Count Bernstorff to King William I, December 6, 1868.

"Mr. Gladstone m'a repondu . . . qu'il fallait naturellement laisser un peu de temps aux Français pour se défaire d'une mauvaise politique traditionelle qui avait voulu que la France ne fut entourée que par des États faibles, et pour s'habituer à avoir des voisins forts, mais qu'ils insultaient eux-mêmes en étant jaloux de l'unité de leurs voisins, puisque, par leur propre magnifique position géographique, l'homogénéité de leur population, la richesse de leur vol et l'esprit militaire de leur peuple, ils étaient bien en état de se défendre contre toute agression du dehors, et n'avaient, par conséquent, à craindre personne." (Ibid., vol. III, p. 64.)

[24] Prince Metternich to Count Beust, December 9, 1868.

"L'Empereur ajouta dans cette conversation que si jamais nous avions à combiner ensemble *une action militaire* quelqu' éloignée qu'elle fusse, il serait très important de s'entendre sur *le terrain militaire,* c'est-à-dire qu'il faudrait *à temps se concerter sur la question stratégique* et ne pas s'abandonner *alors* à des tâtonnements *imprudents*." (Ibid., vol. III, p. 75.)

[25] Count Vitzthum to Count Beust, February 19, 1869.

"Als feststehend kann aber schon jetzt betrachtet werden . . . 2. dass sich Frankreich verpflichtet, uns mit seiner gesamten Macht zu unterstützen, falls wir in Deutschland angegriffen werden oder es überhaupt zum Kriege zwischen uns und Preussen kommt . . . 5. dass, im Falle eines Krieges in Deutschland, beide Mächte oder Frankreich allein, falls es allein engagiert ist, die Waffen nicht eher niederlegen, als bis in Deutschland die Grundlagen eines dauernden Friedens durch Herstellung eines neuen, aus möglichst *gleich mächtigen* Staaten zu bildenden Bundes geschaffen, der Zweck des Krieges sonach erreicht ist; 6. dass alle remaniements territoriaux und compensations d'un commun accord reguliert werden." (Ibid., vol. III, p. 111 f.)

[26] Prince Metternich to Count Beust, March 1, 1869.

"les Germains de leur côté n'y trouveront pas mentionné *le Rhin,* ce que j'ai eu quelque peine à emporter. Ils ne pourront pas se recrier contre une action belliqueuse commune entre nous et l'étranger contre les *deutschen Brüder.*" (Ibid., vol. III, p. 119).

[27] Count Beust to Count Vitzthum, August 26, 1869.

"L'engagement verbal que l'Empereur Napoleon a bien voulu prendre envers notre Ambassadeur, engagement qui nous a été traduit par ces augustes paroles: 'Je considérai ce traité comme s'il était signé' a pu d'autant plus nous nous y repondions et qu'un engagement pareil paraissait indiqué tant qu'aucune des parties contractantes n'énonçait le désir de terminer cette negociation en bonne et due forme." (Ibid., vol. III, p. 224.)

[28] Count Vitzthum to Count Beust, October 7, 1869.

"Sa Majesté . . . aurait resumé Sa manière de voir à

peu près dans ces termes: 'Je suis toujours et plus que jamais dans les mêmes idées, et je considère nos conventions comme moralement signées. Je n'ai pas hésité à m'exprimer dans ce sens tant envers l'Empereur d'Autriche, qu'envers le Roi d'Italie. L'alliance autrichienne forme donc le pivot de ma politique." (Ibid., vol. III, p. 251.)

[29] Emperor Napoleon III to General Lebrun on the plan of war, November, 1869.

"Oh, reprit l'Empereur, on pourrait pourtant établir ce plan sans y faire entrer d'alliances sures ou probables. Mais, au surplus, il serait permis de considérer l'alliance d'Italie, comme certaine, et celle de l'Autriche comme assurée moralement, sinon activement." (Souvenirs militaires du général Lebrun, p. 58 f., Oncken, op. cit., vol. III, p. 268.)

[30] Prince Metternich to Count Beust, January 21, 1870.

"Rouher et Thiers comprennent bien cette situation—*Ollivier les gêne.* Tous les deux ont peur que de grandes choses se passent encore sans eux et par Ollivier. Tous les deux, s'ils revenaient au pouvoir, penseraient à faire la guerre et à prendre le Rhin. Le premier en cherchant à sauver ainsi et à replacer sur le trône autoritaire le '2. Décembre'—Le second pour faire *grand* au profit de sa propre renommée et de sa figure dans l'histoire. Thiers ferait la guerre avec une partie du Ministère actuel et d'après les préceptes constitutionnels, se servant du reste de l'énergie et du prestige que possède encore un Napoléon—Rouher le ferait pour balayer l'opposition et rasseoir son maître." (Ibid., vol. III, p. 295.)

[31] Prince Metternich to Count Beust, January 29, 1870.

"J'ai profité du souper après le bal aux Tuileries pour reconter en peu de mots à l'Empereur ma conversation avec Thiers. Sa Majesté m'a dit: 'Si vraiement Mr. Thiers est *pour la guerre* sous certaines conditions, je le détesterais moins, quant à avoir confiance entière en lui et en ses amis —*c'est plus difficile.'* " (Ibid., vol. III, p. 301.)

[32] Prince Metternich to Count Beust, March 20, 1870.

[Mr. Bethmont, member of the left wing in the Corps Législatif] affirme que malgré cela le cabinet actuel fera de bonnes choses et il m'a dit qu'il lui tardait de prouver ce que la France libre est capable de faire *si elle a le bonheur de jamais marcher avec* Autriche. Voilà le *républicain* qui comme Rouher l'*absolutiste* et Thiers le *parlementaire* pense aussi avec complaisance à une guerre fait en notre compagnie!! Je sais bien que le Rhin est le grand sorcier qui attire la nation—nos beaux yeux y sont pour peu de chose. Raison de plus pour lier notre but d'une facon indissoluble au leur, si jamais la trompette de guerre devrait sonner." (Ibid., vol. III, p. 336.)

[33] Report of General Lebrun on the deliberations of the French council of war on May 19, 1870, with Emperor Napoleon III in the chair.

. . . "L'Empereur exprimait ensuite son opinion personelle, se déclara favorable à un plan de campagne qui reposerait sur les données suivantes. . . . La guerre étant declarée, trois armées, de 100,000 hommes chacune, l'une française, une autre autrichienne et la troisième italienne, envahiraient aussitôt la territoire du midi de l'Allemagne. Les trois armées auraient pour premier objectif un point central du territoire de ces Etats. Elles s'y concentreraient sous le commandement d'un généralissime designé d'avance par les trois souverains intéressés. Sur les 300,000 hommes réunis ainsi, un corps de 30 a 40,000 Italiens serait jeté à Munich pour occuper, en permanence, cette capitale de la Bavière. Au moyen de ces premières dispositions, on pouvait espérer que l'on détacherait de la Prusse les forces de la Bavière, du Wurtemberg et du Grand-Duché de Bade

. . . Ce premier résultat obtenu, l'armée alliée, diminuée des 40,000 Italiens laissés a Munich, se dirigerait vers le haut Mein pour aller prendre pied en Franconie et s'y établir sur une base d'operations s'entendant de Würtzbourg à Nuremberg ou Amberg. C'est de cette base qu'elle partirait ensuite pour commencer les grandes operations de la campagne." (Ibid., vol. III, p. 361.)

[34] Prince Metternich to Count Beust, July 8, 1870.

"J'ai trouvé mercredi dernier l'Empereur très occupé de l'affaire Hohenzollern. Il avait l'air enchanté, je dirais même *joyeusement monté.* Il m'aborda avec la phrase devenue sacramentelle: 'Eh bien que dites-Vous de notre affaire?' . . . L'Empereur se recria en me disant: 'Croyez-vous vraiement qu'en face de la mise en demeura très energique que nous leur avons adressée et dont le Duc de Gramont à ce moment même donne l'interpretation très vigoureuse à la Chambre on puisse ceder immédiatement à Berlin?' " (Ibid., vol. III, p. 400.)

[35] Prince Metternich to Count Beust, July 8, 1870.

"J'ai trouvé l'Impératrice tellement montée en faveur de la guerre que je n'ai pas pu m'empecher de la plaisanter un peu . . . 'Mais il est inutile de parler de cette éventualité,' ajouta l'Impératrice. 'Il sera fort difficile à Mr. de Bismarck de s'en tirer sans nous ceder rendement ou sans avouer la chose. S'il cède, ce ne sera que devant notre attitude comminatoire, une humiliation dont il ne se relève que difficilement et dont, croyez-le bien, nous ne lui saurons aucun gré.' " (Ibid., vol. III, p. 401 f.)

[36] Prince Metternich to Count Beust, July 8, 1870.

"Mr. Ollivier revenait de la Chambre où le discours qu'il avait rédigé et fait lire par le Duc de Gramont avait eu un succès frénétique. Il en était très heureux et semblait fort monté en me débitant son discours: 'Nous en avons assez' me dit-il, 'des humiliations que la Prusse veut nous imposer.

Ce ne sont plus des Rouher ou des La Valette qui ont à diriger la politique de la France. C'est moi, un ministre du peuple, sortant du peuple, sentant avec le peuple, moi, un ministre responsable devant la nation, responsable de sa dignité et devant couvrir l'Empereur, qui ai mené cette affaire avec la révolution patriotique que Vous me connaissez. Plus d'hésitations, plus de tergiversations, le conseil a été unanime. Nous avons décidé comme un seul homme qu'il fallait marcher, nous avons entrainé la Chambre, nous entrainerons la nation. Dans quinze jours nous aurons 400,000 hommes sur la Saar et cette fois-ci nous ferons la guerre comme en 93, nous armerons le peuple qui courra aux frontières.' " (Ibid., vol. III, p. 402 f.)

[37] Prince Metternich to Count Beust, July 8, 1870.

"Le Ministre des Affaires étrangères a déclaré au Conseil des Ministres sur une question que lui a adressée le Ministre de la guerre que selon renseignements, puises à bonne source, l'Autriche en cas de guerre enverrait un corps d'observation sur la frontière et paralyserait ainsi une partie des forces prussiennes. . . . Je lui ai dit: Vous avez simplement sauté de pieds joints sur une occasion, vu le proverbe, qu'une bonne occasion ne se retrouve plus. Vous avez pensé qu'il fallait la prendre aux cheveux pour obtenir ou un succès diplomatique dont Vous croyez avoir besoin, ou pour faire la guerre sur un terrain qui ne puisse mettre contre Vous l'esprit national allemand. 'C'est parfaitement dit et je ne demande pas mieux,' me repondit le Duc, 'que Vous mettiez le Chancelier dans la confidence du coup de dé.' 'Mr. de Beust,' ajouta-t-il, 'doit ailleurs être content de moi, il devait s'attendre à *un coup de ma facon.*' " (Ibid., vol. III, p. 405.)

[38] Prince Metternich to Count Beust, July 11, 1870.

"Duc de Gramont est un peu en contradiction avec Mr. Ollivier qui voudrait d'autres questions à celle de Hohenzollern pour rendre la guerre inévitable, tandis que Gramont veut la paix si le Roi de Prusse cède." (Ibid., vol. III, p. 417.)

[39] Prince Metternich to Count Beust, July 12, 1870.

"L'Empereur m'a demandé si je ne croyais pas qu'il ne faut pas compliquer la question. J'ai encouragé fortement Sa Majesté à ne pas le faire. Empereur Napoleon essayera d'un nouveau moyen. Il décrétera demain, mardi, la mobilisation au premier degré sans changer l'état de la question et croit que cela rendra la guerre inévitable." (Ibid., vol. III, p. 427.)

[40] The Danish minister Count Moltke-Hvitfeldt to the Minister of Foreign Affairs Baron Rosenörn-Lehn, July 18, 1870.

"Avant de quitter le ministre [Duke of Gramont] il nous dit qu'il croyait que les deux armées ennemies seraient fortement engagées d'ici à quinze jours. 'Nous avons,' nous dit-il, 'dix de quinze jours d'avance sur les Prussiens en ce qui concerne les préparatifs militaires; nous en aurions eu davantage si nous avions pu, ainsi que nous le désirions, prolonger la durée des negotiations; malheureusement il y a eu insulte de la parte du Roi de Prusse et ce fait a nécessairement eu pour résultat de faire cesser instantanément tous les pourparlers!" (Ibid., vol. III, p. 456 f.)

[41] Duke of Gramont to Count Beust, July 17, 1870.

"Si j'avais pu choisir l'heure de l'action, je n'aurais certes pas manque de parfaire nos traités et d'établir, tout à notre aise, pour vous comme pour nous, l'accord que je vous demand aujourd'hui de faire bien à la hâte . . . Si vous nous laissez seuls, la campagne sera nécessairement courte, quoique brillante, et stérile dans ses résultats definitifs. Si vous nous aidez, si, permettant à l'Italie de porter 70 à 80,000 hommes en Bavière, par votre territoire, vous en envoyez 150,000 en Bohème et mettez plus tard sur pied 2 à 300,000 hommes, c'est à Berlin que la paix se signe et que vous effacez d'un trait glorieux tous les souvenirs et toutes les conséquences de 1866. Jamais pareille occasion ne se présentera de nouveau; jamais vous ne trouverez un concours aussi réel, jamais la France ne sera aussi forte qu'aujourd'hui, jamais mieux armée, mieux équipée, ni animée d'un plus grand enthousiasme." (Ibid., vol. III, p. 452 f.)

[42] Prince Reuss to Bismarck, St. Petersburg, August 12, 1870.

"Aus ganz sicherer Quelle, aber nicht durch den Fürsten Gortschakoff erfahre ich folgendes. Vor dem Tage von Weissenburg (4. Aug.) hat der Herzog von Gramont dem russischen Geschäftsträger in detaillierter Weise Mitteilung von den Bedingungen gemacht, unter denen Frankreich bereit sein würde, in *Berlin* den Frieden zu diktieren. Als Minimum der Forderungen würde betrachtet: 1. Reduktion Preussens auf seine Grenzen von 1866. 2. Abtretung des Saar-Kohlenbeckens an Frankreich. 3. Zahlung der Kriegskosten an Frankreich und Restituierung der Kriegskosten an Österreich. 4. Wiederherstellung der Depossedierten. 5. Vergrösserung der Mittelstaaten auf Kosten von preussischem Gebiet. 6. Konstituierung von Staatengruppen in Deutschland, welche die preussische Suprematie dauernd brechen würden. Ferner hat der französische Minister dem russischen Geschäftsträger aufgetragen, sein Gouvernement zu sondieren, was Russland tun würde, wenn die französische Armee in Berlin stünde, und Russland für die Neutralität Danzig angeboten." (Ibid., vol. III, p. 526 f.)